HAPPY HOUR SNACKS

BEC VRANA DICKINSON

PHOTOGRAPHY BY **CHRIS CHEN**

Hardie Grant

BOOKS

This book was written on Bidjigal, Birrabirragal and Gadigal
Country, home of the Eora Nation, the traditional custodians
of this land and these waterways and seas.

I pay my respects to Elders, past and present and I acknowledge
that the land I live and work on was stolen. This place is home
to one of the oldest surviving cultures.

This always was and always will be Aboriginal land.

CONTENTS

YOU'RE A BIT SALTY

12

THE SPICE AND SMOKE SHOW

54

HOW GOOD IS ACID?

96

CHEESE SLEAZE

136

AFTERS, ALWAYS.

176

COOKING ICE

Scene 1:

A discussion is heard over speakerphone.
Emily and Bec are housemates and their friend
Kate lives nearby.

                     KATE
        'Yoooo, I'm heading over now ...'

[Kate's actually still at home.]

                    EMILY
        'Sweeeeet! The door is open ...'

                     KATE
        'Roger that. I've got us all a
        HOT little tequila. You got the
        ice cooking?'

                    EMILY
        'Sorted — got two trays
        simmering.'

                     KATE
        'Of course you do. Want chips ...?'

[Hearing this, Bec yells to the phone:]

        'Err — YEAH WE DO!'

[Still yelling ...]

        'WE ALSO PICKED SOME FRESH
        SIDEWALK HERBS, PERFECT FOR ...'

This book. THIS fucking book.

[The reader reads on ...]

MORE THAN HUMMUS, LESS THAN ARANCINI

I'm no snack prophet. I'm not trying to turn water into wine, I just like this ritual of snacking and sipping in tandem. And I like you, because you like dips, chips and drinks. That's why you're here, right? So, pull up a pew (or stool, or floor cushion) and let's hang.

We're not at a wine bar with all the etiquette and arancini. We're at home, and constricting denim is optional. It is looser, lazier and louder. Plus, you can lick your fingers with *even more* abandon. We're happy to be here.

To all the tubs of hummus, bunches of grapes and charcuterie boards: I see you and I appreciate you. Thing is, I just need some more fireworks …

Here, it's more about dressing up tater tots and rethinking dips, and less about all the bowls, utensils and faff. Because washing up sucks (especially the morning after), and the only thing we want to suck is … olives. Many, many juicy olives.

THE STICKY FINGERS MANTRA

From now on, when I say 'snack', I'm referring to your own independently constructed mouthfuls. We're not labouring over canapés, stacking things onto skewers (except on page 91), or acrobatically balancing little bits on bigger bits. This is the definition of DIY: grab a fork or use your fingers (personal preference) to pile and arrange your own damn cracker. Keep napkins and tea towels close by; any wiping materials will be well received.

The breakdown

This book is split into five cravings:

- You're a bit salty (salt)
- The spice and smoke show (spice and smoke)
- How good is acid? (zest and tang)
- Cheese sleaze (cheese)
- Afters, always. (sweets)

Stick with one, or blend and shake.

Each recipe comes with a drink pairing proposal. For the record, these are not sommelier-grade recs, they're more drink-meets-food-meets-yeah-I'd-enjoy-those-together thoughts. See these drinks as an opportunity to broaden and flex your bar cart. A quick web search will provide the drinks recipes, if you need. But feel free to go your own way with this. You're an adult, so pick your own battles, bottles and alcohol content, if any. There's a glass (or can) for everyone to hold.

The snack serving size is an estimate, because I can't speak for your stomach. Three recipes (roughly) should comfortably satiate a crowd. Also, if you're like me and have an inherent fear of under-catering, don't be afraid to lean on plenty of *good* bread and room-temperature butter for a bit of extra padding – it's rarely needed, but it sets the mind at ease.

Living with my housemate, dear Emily, our gluten-intolerant champion, I have made sure these recipes can also be adapted to avoid gluten. Considering different sensitivities and preferences (gluten, dairy, nut, vegetarian and vegan), dietary flags and swaps are noted, too. Just trade in suitable bread, or swap peanuts for cashews (Em's allergic to those too). Let's keep our friends alive.

In terms of commitment, I'm not sure where you sit on the scale, but here, there's no mixed messages. Just pick your time-commitment category:

- Quickie
- Minor investment
- Go the distance

There's a mixture in each chapter, and each has its own merits. If you like, shave off some minutes by using pre-chopped ingredients (e.g. trading garlic, ginger and chilli for pre-made pastes). In the spirit of convenience, and speaking as a non-dishwasher owner, we're aiming for fewer dishes by avoiding hectic equipment like food processors (handy, but ... that blade).

These recipes just need a simple board, bowl and knife (you'll see I'm also partial to scissors). Or, of course, hands. We mix sauces in their serving bowls, and even in their tubs. We win. Soap suds lose.

Before you hit the store, I want to reassure you that there are no more than fifteen ingredients per recipe (some are even dangerously below that number). If you can't find the exact ingredient or would rather rummage through your fridge, look down to *THE SUBS, because not everyone should have to suffer through my tarragon addiction. En route down the ingredient list, you'll also meet the toppers, scoopers and dippers (I trust these are self-explanatory). Their quantities are deliberately non-specific; forget the scales for garnishes. We're at the finish line and we just want to eat.

Each chapter also has a little something extra for you to try. Lean all the way in with a micro-challenge (mostly for group events) or peel it back and try the '4 ways' to approach some classics (made for the endearingly lazy and last-minute folks). As the chefs, we sometimes forget to drink on shift – that's why there are batch cocktails. Meaning, if everyone else is getting a glass, so do you.

How lush and plush you want to go with these snacks is up to you. Go for the hand-wrapped deli cheese or just the supermarket stuff – it's all gravy, baby. I've tested it, and it all works. Either way, you're making an effort, so hats off.

Foresight, for now

The majority of these recipes have been cooked off the cuff. As in, me in a bath towel. My friends, Sush and Paddy, on their way over. My hands smelling of garlic. Did I get the dill? The floor is wet. That bottle needs chilling. Is my top clean? But it all works out, really. They don't care, and it turns out they have dill.

In saying this, preparation rules – preparation SAVES! On better days, I'm already showered and I give myself a little checklist (optional). I'm not sweaty. I sit on the couch with my friends and put my clean feet up on the coffee table. Feels good.

Try to conquer the small things early: toast nuts, pre-mix dips, boil eggs, chop herbs and slice bread. It all helps. I even occasionally lay out the plates I want to use and label what they should hold. It's a little excessive, but it's a visual help.

Scrappy is good

Sometimes you'll lick the plate clean, other times there will be scraps (the good kind). Use leftover sauces in soups and sandwiches, or loosen with olive oil and water to make dressings. Melt cheese over your next roast. Fry bread into crusty croutons and toss into salads. Freeze things then turn them into your next meal topped with your favourite form of egg. You deserve it.

Note: This book uses 250 ml (8½ fl oz) cup measures and 20 ml (¾ fl oz) tablespoons. Oven temperatures are for conventional settings.

YOU'RE A BIT SALTY

I'm happy to be salty. Make it my second name and roll me in that white dust.

Let me explain salting. (It's only my favourite topic.) Picture the process like a bell curve: as you add more, the flavour rises until you hit that thigh-slapping peak. That's elation. But adding too much salt can tip it back down again. Be too heavy-handed and saltiness can quickly slip into thirst.

In saying that, trust your salting hand, because balance can usually be restored. If needed, just add a splash of acid (e.g. lemon juice or vinegar), a bit of something sweet (e.g. honey or sugar) and, if the circumstances are right, a dollop of dairy (e.g. yoghurt or cream). Taste as you go.

Keep in mind that saltiness comes in many forms before you even hit the salt itself – think fish sauce, cheese, capers, anchovies, olives and cured meats. You'll try them all here. It'll get personal.

One final word: we're all different. It's always a good idea to leave a bowl of salt on the table to let others sort their own bell curve out.

FRIENDLY ANCHOVIES

DF / GF / NF

This is not about the strongly salted tiny brown variety of anchovies that, truthfully, disappears into sauces (I choose not to believe anything else). These white ones (boquerones) are marinated in salt, vinegar and oil, so they're mild and delicate, but still bring the salt.

Know someone who doesn't like anchovies? Perfect – make them try one of these. If they still don't like them, enjoy a bonus expression of disgust. We're not here to make friends, just to tease them.

DRINK CAVA
SNACKS 4–6
COMMITMENT QUICKIE

2 oranges
120 g (4½ oz) boquerones (white anchovies)
1 ripe avocado, peeled, stone removed, sliced
3 radishes, trimmed, thinly sliced into rounds
 or wedges

TOPPERS
snipped chives
drizzle of honey
drizzle of garlic oil

SCOOPERS
(preferably) cracked black pepper potato chips

Cut around the oranges to remove the skin, then slice into rounds, or you can try segmenting.

Be crafty: layer the boquerones, avocado, radish and orange in a cool way. Top with the chives. Give it a good season, then drizzle with honey and garlic oil.

Stack or scoop with chips.

✱ THE SUBS
 ORANGES mandarin / blood orange / pomelo
 CHIVES parsley / basil
 GARLIC OIL extra-virgin olive oil

PIP SUCKER

DF / VEG / VEGAN

Want to look busy? Suck an olive.

Don't want to talk? Suck an olive.

Snacky?! Suck. An. Olive.

And make eye contact.

Let this be the genesis of your olive-warming. If you want to feel extra expensive, use good-quality extra-virgin olive oil because you'll be soaking it all up with bread. For when you're tired of sucking.

DRINK APEROL SPRITZ
SNACKS 4-6
COMMITMENT QUICKIE

1 orange
3 garlic cloves, peeled
125 ml (4 fl oz/½ cup) extra-virgin olive oil
1 teaspoon caraway seeds
a few rosemary and oregano sprigs
300 g (10½ oz) mixed olives

TOPPERS
smoked almonds

DIPPERS
fresh bread

Peel 3–4 strips of orange rind with a vegetable peeler. Smash the garlic – the side of a knife works well.

To a small saucepan, add the oil, orange rind, garlic, caraway seeds and herbs. Heat over a low heat to infuse, around 8–10 minutes.

Now stir in the olives and leave on the heat until they're warmed through. It should only take a few minutes.

Tip the olives (right away!) into a serving bowl. Top with or serve alongside smoked almonds, and soak up the oil with the bread.

✱ THE SUBS
  ORANGE lemon
  CARAWAY SEEDS fennel seeds / cumin seeds / anise seeds
  ROSEMARY AND OREGANO thyme / marjoram / bay leaves
  SMOKED ALMONDS any roasted almond or nut

BETTER BUTTER

NF

Like most good things, bottarga isn't the prettiest. Don't let that deter you from gripping and grating it. The dried and salted pouches of fish roe are like the parmesan of the sea. Coming in large-ish pieces, you're likely to have some left over, so please grate that over some pasta and call me over.

Specialist Italian grocers are your best bet for bottarga, but if you can't find it there, make this with anchovies instead. Or, if you want to head in a more ornate direction, use caviar. Keep it classy and call the veg' sticks 'crudité'. Are we fancy yet?

Also, the whipped butter isn't friends with the fridge. Just whip and serve. Simple.

DRINK CHARDONNAY
SNACKS 6–8
COMMITMENT QUICKIE

150 g (5½ oz) salted butter,
    at room temperature
50 g (1¾ oz) bottarga

SCOOPERS
1 small fennel bulb
bunch of radishes, trimmed
bunch of baby carrots
sourdough breadsticks

TOPPERS
extra-virgin olive oil
mixed sesame seeds

Prep the scoopers: wash the veg, then thinly slice the fennel, quarter the radishes, halve or quarter the carrots lengthways and slice or tear the sourdough. Lay out on a platter.

Add the butter to a bowl and beat with an electric mixer for a good 4 minutes, or until really light and fluffy.

Dollop the butter high (or smear it) in a serving bowl. Drizzle the oil over the butter. Grate over the bottarga and top with the sesame seeds.

Serve with the crudité.

* **THE SUBS**
    BOTTARGA anchovies / caviar
    VEG' SCOOPERS cucumber / chicory (endive) /
    sugar-snap peas / capsicum (bell pepper)

SO PUFFED

NF

Sandwiching the puff pastry between baking trays will help control the puff here and form a more cracker-like thickness. You'll also get to enjoy a 'ta-dah!' moment when you pull the top tray off. Say it with me, 'I am a magician.'

Also, consider puff pastry your kitchen perfume. Cook it to cover any odd lingering smells.

DRINK OLD FASHIONED
SNACKS 4-6
COMMITMENT QUICKIE

2 sheets puff pastry
sprinkle of sea salt flakes
sprinkle of nigella seeds
1 pear, thinly sliced
100 g (3½ oz) bresaola
100 g (3½ oz) ricotta salata

TOPPERS
truffle oil

Preheat the oven to 200°C (390°F). Line a baking tray with baking paper.

Cut the pastry into long thin strips or triangles, or any fun lengthy character.

Sprinkle over some sea salt and nigella seeds. Top with another sheet of baking paper and a heavy baking tray (or two) to weigh the pastry down. Bake until golden and just a little puffed, 15–20 minutes.

Arrange the pear, bresaola and ricotta salata on a board with a little knife on the side. Add your homemade puffs. Stack them up and drizzle some truffle oil over the top.

✱ THE SUBS
NIGELLA SEEDS caraway seeds / fennel seeds / sesame seeds
PEAR fig / peach / grape / dried apricot
BRESAOLA prosciutto
RICOTTA SALATA feta
TRUFFLE OIL truffle honey / truffle paste

PERKY PRETZELS

NF

Baked pretzels sometimes go stale faster than you can conquer them. To revive, douse them under running water then give them a blast in a hot oven. It does feel a little weird to treat a pretzel like a sink-side sponge, but it works. In fact, you can do this with any stale bread. How neat!

DRINK BOCK
SNACKS 2–4
COMMITMENT QUICKIE

2 baked salted pretzels
2 tablespoons extra-virgin olive oil, plus a little extra for drizzling
1 tablespoon caraway seeds
2 tablespoons wholegrain mustard
250 g (9 oz) crème fraîche
small bunch of tarragon, chopped
small bunch of dill, chopped

TOPPERS
sauerkraut
Swiss cheese
pastrami

Preheat the oven to 220°C (430°F). Line a baking tray with baking paper.

Place the pretzels on the baking tray, evenly pour the oil on top and rub to coat. Sprinkle the caraway seeds evenly over the pretzels. Bake until warmed and golden, about 5 minutes.

Meanwhile, combine the mustard, crème fraîche and herbs in a serving bowl. Stir, then season and top with an extra drizzle of olive oil.

Serve the pretzels with the dip, sauerkraut, Swiss cheese and pastrami.

✱ THE SUBS
CARAWAY SEEDS fennel seeds / cumin seeds
WHOLEGRAIN MUSTARD dijon mustard / English mustard
CRÈME FRAÎCHE sour cream / cream cheese
TARRAGON AND DILL chervil / parsley / chives
SWISS CHEESE gouda / cheddar / havarti / gruyere

FRENCH-FRIED SCALLOPS

GF / NF

It's time to get PRO at pat-drying your PROteins. Meaning meats, fish, tofu, blah blah – I know you know. This removes excess moisture. Less moisture means less liquid evaporating as you cook, meaning more time for the protein to actually caramelise and brown, achieving a true sear.

DRINK MANZANILLA SHERRY
SNACKS 4–6
COMMITMENT QUICKIE

½ bunch of curly parsley
2 tablespoons extra-virgin olive oil
16 scallops, shelled
80 g (2¾ oz) butter
2 garlic cloves, sliced
2 tablespoons fish sauce
½ bunch of dill, roughly chopped
zest and juice of 1 lemon

TOPPERS
packet of French Fries chips (crisps)
shaved parmesan
lemon wedges

Finely chop the parsley stems and roughly chop the leaves.

Heat the oil in a large frying pan over a medium–high heat and leave for a few minutes to warm up. Pat the scallops dry with paper towel, then cook for 2–3 minutes each side, or until golden, being wary not to crowd the pan. Move the scallops to a serving plate.

Add the butter to the pan and scrape the base to release any leftover scallop-y bits. Leave the butter to foam, about 2 minutes, then add the garlic. Stir until smelling nutty and garlicky, around another 2 minutes. Remove from the heat.

Stir in the fish sauce, parsley, dill, lemon zest and a good squeeze of lemon juice. Give everything a little season, then pour the butter sauce over the scallops.

Top the scallops with French Fries and parmesan. Serve with lemon wedges. Skewer or fork them. Extra French fries on the side.

✱ THE SUBS
  CURLY PARSLEY flat-leaf (Italian) parsley / chives / extra dill
  FISH SAUCE soy sauce / miso paste
  DILL chives / extra parsley
  FRENCH FRIES CHIPS crushed chips (crisps)

SALAMI NAPKINS

NF

Salami is your main mode of transport here. Use the meaty rounds to scoop and wrap up the crunchy topping. If you want to feel fancy, call the bread topping a 'pangrattato' and use forks.

DRINK SANGIOVESE
SNACKS 6-8
COMMITMENT MINOR INVESTMENT

2 tablespoons extra-virgin olive oil,
  plus a little extra for drizzling
2 × 100 g (3½ oz) slices sourdough bread,
  torn into small chunks
2 garlic cloves, crushed or finely chopped
zest of 1 lemon
80 g (2¾ oz) sultanas
350 g (12½ oz) goat's cheese
100 g (3½ oz) fennel salami, thinly sliced
120 g (4½ oz) pitted green olives, torn or sliced

Heat the oil in a large frying pan over a medium–high heat and fry the bread until golden.

Add the garlic and toss to unlock the smell. Take the pan off the heat and mix in the lemon zest and sultanas. Havea little bready nibble and season.

Spread the goat's cheese over a serving plate. Fold the salami on top to look all three-dimensional (or keep on the side). Scatter over the toasty bread and olives. Scoop it all up with the salami.

✱ THE SUBS
  SOURDOUGH bread of choice
  GOAT'S CHEESE labneh / feta
  FENNEL SALAMI salami of choice
  GREEN OLIVES kalamata olives / marinated artichokes / capers

CROISSANT CHIPS

NF

I was late to ham. The soft and salty pork only spoke to me during an off-chance meeting and eating one Christmas with hot English mustard. It made a mockery of me, and I was converted. Now, ham and cheese is my croissant of choice. So mature! So ... that's my relationship history with ham.

You could also make this vegetarian and swap the ham for some mushrooms (pan-fried in butter, thyme and garlic would be nice). I think I might try that too now. To be clear, I STILL LOVE HAM.

DRINK VIOGNIER
SNACKS 4–6
COMMITMENT MINOR INVESTMENT

2 croissants
2 heaped tablespoons wholegrain mustard
100 g (3½ oz) cream cheese
100 g (3½ oz) shaved leg ham
100 g (3½ oz) Swiss cheese, shaved or grated
1 tablespoon poppy seeds

TOPPERS
chives
caramelised onions

Preheat the oven grill (broiler) to high. Line a baking tray with foil.

Thinly slice the croissants into rounds and spread out on the tray. Grill until golden, keeping an eye on them, for about 4 minutes.

Meanwhile, combine the mustard and cream cheese in a bowl. Give it a season.

Once the croissants are toasted, spread the cream cheese mix over the slices (you can be slapdash). Tear over the leg ham and top with the cheese. Sprinkle with the poppy seeds.

Grill until the cheese is melted and golden brown, about 8 minutes.

Snip over some chives. Serve with caramelised onions nearby or top with instead, up to you.

✱ **THE SUBS**
WHOLEGRAIN MUSTARD dijon mustard / hot English mustard
CREAM CHEESE crème fraîche / sour cream
SWISS CHEESE gouda / cheddar / gruyere
POPPY SEEDS sesame seeds / nigella seeds

PAPPADUM CHIPPIES

GF / NF / VEG

Saving room for the full meal is futile when pappadums hit the table. With a side of chutney and yoghurt, none of this lasts long. You dip! You crunch! You whet! Your! Appetite!

DRINK GINGER BEER
SNACKS 4-6
COMMITMENT MINOR INVESTMENT

60 ml (2 fl oz/¼ cup) neutral oil,
    like vegetable or sunflower
4 curry leaf sprigs, leaves picked
120 g (4½ oz) ready-to-eat pappadums
1 tablespoon curry powder
300 g (10½ oz) Greek yoghurt

TOPPERS
mango chutney
coriander (cilantro)

Preheat the oven to 220°C (430°F). Line a baking tray with baking paper.

Heat the oil in a large frying pan over a high heat. Have a piece of paper towel laid out nearby. When the oil has a real good quiver, get the tongs – this will happen fast.

Fry the curry leaves in the hot oil until crisp, around 20 seconds, then transfer them to the paper towel. Take the oil off the heat to cool a little.

Spread the pappadums over the baking tray. Stir the curry powder into the oil and pour over the pappadums. Toss and rub to coat, let them break them up a little – it's fun, get your hands in there.

Bake the pappadums until properly golden and fragrant, about 5 minutes. Remove from the oven, give everything a little season, then leave to cool and crisp up.

Spoon the yoghurt into a bowl and top with some mango chutney. Give it a good season and little swirl. Top with torn coriander and fried curry leaves.

Scoop the yoghurt with the pappadums and be on your way.

* THE SUBS
CORIANDER mint
MANGO CHUTNEY any fruity chutney /
tomato kasundi

B.L.T X C.SAR

NF

DRINK PIMM'S
SNACKS 6–8
COMMITMENT MINOR INVESTMENT

150 g (5½ oz) bacon rashers (slices)
bunch of chives, chopped
bunch of dill, chopped
80 g (2¾ oz) gherkins, chopped
1 tablespoon anchovy paste
150 g (5½ oz) garlic aioli
150 g (5½ oz) sour cream
1 tablespoon dijon mustard
½ rotisserie chicken
100 g (3½ oz) grated parmesan

TOPPERS
extra-virgin olive oil, for drizzling

SCOOPERS
cos (romaine) lettuce wedges
pan-fried bread (see method), optional
celery stalks

Who? Rotisserie chicken.

What? The stuffing.

Where? A supermarket. Follow your nose.

Why? The juice at the bottom of the bag.

How? With your fingers.

I don't need love letters, I just need rotisserie chicken on a Sunday to shred, gnaw and suck, then lick all the flavour off my fingers. That's how I sleep tight.

Heat a large frying pan over a medium heat. Add the bacon and fry, turning regularly, until golden and proper crisp, around 5–8 minutes. Chop roughly and set aside. If you're frying your bread for scooping, do that now. Slice the bread. Place the frying pan back over a medium heat and drizzle a little olive oil over the bread slices. Fry in the residual bacon fat until golden on both sides, then cut in half lengthways and season with salt. Set aside.

Combine the herbs, gherkin, anchovy paste, aioli, sour cream, dijon and chopped bacon in a large dipping bowl.

Pull, shred and tear the chicken straight into a bowl. Add the stuffing, if any, the parmesan and some freshly cracked black pepper. Give it a good mix to combine and top with a drizzle of olive oil.

Scoop with the lettuce, fried bread and celery.

✱ THE SUBS
CHIVES AND DILL parsley / mint / basil / tarragon
GHERKINS capers
GARLIC AIOLI your mayo' of choice
SOUR CREAM cream cheese / crème fraîche
DIJON MUSTARD wholegrain mustard /
hot English mustard
PAN-FRIED BREAD fresh or toasted bread

PIGGY BAR MIX

Want a fun little group conversation question?
Sure you do …

'What's your favourite nut, and why?'

I'm serious. This is creative freedom! Do you like them salted, roasted or both? How about crushed? Tell me. I was shocked to hear my friend Sush's was a brazil nut. But am I really? No – she likes to be different. She owns an Android. Mine? Well, this month it's roasted almonds, skin on, roughly chopped, for every meal.

How great is this chat?

P.S. Regarding this actual recipe, don't bother with the extra pig (prosciutto) if an extra tray is a tray too many.

DRINK STOUT
SNACKS 6-8
COMMITMENT MINOR INVESTMENT

1 teaspoon cayenne pepper
2 tablespoons fennel seeds
60 ml (2 fl oz/¼ cup) extra-virgin olive oil
2 tablespoons honey
2 teaspoons sea salt flakes
100 g (3½ oz) prosciutto
80 g (2¾ oz) pretzels
150 g (5½ oz) mixed nuts
4 rosemary sprigs, torn
1 tablespoon smoked paprika
60 g (2 oz) grated parmesan
50 g (1¾ oz) pork crackles

Preheat the oven to 220°C (430°F). Line two baking trays with baking paper.

Combine the cayenne pepper, fennel seeds, oil, honey and salt in a bowl with a gooood crack of black pepper.

Spread the prosciutto (decently spaced to help it crisp) over one baking tray. Spread the pretzels and nuts over the other. Toss the spiced oil mix through the nut mix.

Bake both the nut mix and prosciutto, tossing both occasionally, until the prosciutto is proper crisp and the nuts are toasted, about 10 minutes. Let the prosciutto cool.

Sprinkle the rosemary, paprika and parmesan over the nuts, toss to coat, then return to the oven and toast again until the parmesan is golden and crisp, about 2–3 minutes. Remove from the oven and make sure the mixture is well spread out so it can cool (this ensures maximum crunch).

Break the prosciutto over the nut mix. Add the crackles and toss. Bowl it, or refrigerate if making ahead (well done you).

✱ THE SUBS
CAYENNE PEPPER chilli powder / chilli flakes
FENNEL SEEDS caraway seeds / cumin seeds
PROSCIUTTO bacon / pancetta
ROSEMARY thyme
PARMESAN pecorino / cheddar

TARAMA WITH CRUNCHY KALAMATAS

NF

Tiny herb jars are cute and all, but have you ever scrunched the leaves straight off a bunch of dried oregano from Greece? It adds a worthy tactile edge. Have a hunt around. These bunches are usually available at big supermarkets, delis and speciality grocers. Use them here, in your weekly bolognese batch, over buttery potatoes, with honey and haloumi, or just hang it in your kitchen to look pretty.

DRINK OUZO MARTINI
SNACKS 4-6
COMMITMENT MINOR INVESTMENT

140 g (5 oz) pitted kalamata olives
25 g (1 oz) panko breadcrumbs
1 tablespoon dried oregano
2 tablespoons garlic oil, plus extra for drizzling
150 g (5½ oz) Greek yoghurt
50 g (1¾ oz) feta
zest and juice of 1 lemon
small bunch of dill, chopped
400 g (14 oz) taramasalata
freshly cracked pepper, to taste

SCOOPERS
toasted pita bread
baby cucumbers, quartered

Preheat the oven to 220°C (430°F). Line a baking tray with baking paper.

Spread the olives on the tray. Top with the breadcrumbs, oregano and garlic oil. Toss and scrunch to make sure the olives are well coated in the oil and breadcrumbs. Bake for 8–10 minutes, or until golden, tossing halfway through.

In a serving bowl, combine the yoghurt, feta, a good squeeze of lemon juice and most of the dill. Give it a good season and mix well. Add the taramasalata and vaguely swirl the two dips together.

Toss the lemon zest through the crunchy kalamatas and arrange over the dip. Drizzle with some extra garlic oil. Top with the remaining dill and some freshly cracked pepper. Scoop away with the pita and cucumber.

* THE SUBS
KALAMATA OLIVES any pitted olives
PANKO BREADCRUMBS coarse breadcrumbs / bread blitzed or torn into small pieces
GARLIC OIL extra-virgin olive oil
DILL mint / parsley

MISO BUTTER BOIL-OS

GF / NF

I get worked up when it comes to the 'how do you like your eggs?' chat. In a *tell me how you like your eggs and I'll tell you about yourself* kind of way. One ingredient, many possibilities, many personalities.

I'm in strong favour of boil-os (forget poached, I'll reason with you another day). Despite their obvious ease, there's also a lot of cooking-style variables that can enter the chat (time, when the water boils, etc.), but I don't want to complicate things. It's not necessary.

We're boiling for just over seven minutes, hoping for a jammy yolk, but you can also cook to your timing preference. Don't go getting worked up over it.

DRINK RICE LAGER
SNACKS 8–12
COMMITMENT GO THE DISTANCE

12 eggs (older eggs are easier to peel)
100 g (3½ oz) butter
3 cm (1¼ in) piece ginger, peeled and grated
2 garlic cloves, thinly sliced
2 long red chillies, thinly sliced
2 spring onions (scallions), thinly sliced
1 tablespoon white miso paste
1 tablespoon rice vinegar

TOPPERS
mixed sesame seeds
bonito flakes

Bring a large saucepan of water to the boil over a high heat. Cook the eggs in the boiling water for seven and a half minutes. Drain and run under cold water. (Plunge into iced water if you want to be exact.)

In a frying pan, melt the butter over a medium–high heat until it starts to brown. First it will foam for a while, so you've got time. Add the ginger, garlic, chilli and the white ends of the spring onions. Swirl and cook until the butter is brown and smells nutty. Take off the heat.

Stir the miso paste and rice vinegar into the butter until well combined. It will need a good smudging with the back of a spoon. Taste to see if salt is needed.

Peel the eggs, hopefully with ease, then slice in half.

Plate the eggs, yolk side-up, then spoon the miso butter on top. Scatter with the sesame seeds, remaining green spring onion and the bonito flakes.

Eat with fingers, spoons or teeny-tiny toasts.

✱ THE SUBS
WHITE MISO PASTE splash of soy sauce
BONITO FLAKES roasted seaweed snacks / furikake / fried shallots

TOP TOTS

GF / NF

'Gimme some of your tots' is what I almost named this recipe. Because as much as I try, I can't shake the thought of Napoleon Dynamite sitting in school with tots crammed into his pants zipper pocket. The ingenuity.

Unlike Napoleon's cafeteria tots, these are fancied-up with ease. But with the sour cream sauce they may not be fit for a small pants pocket … I'll pay you to try.

DRINK LEMON GIN SPRITZ
SNACKS 6–8
COMMITMENT GO THE DISTANCE

60 ml (2 fl oz/¼ cup) extra-virgin olive oil
50 g (1¾ oz) capers, drained and rinsed
1 kg (2 lb 3 oz) frozen potato gems (tater tots)
2 lemons
360 g (12½ oz) sour cream
2 tablespoons horseradish cream
bunch of chives, chopped
bunch of dill, chopped
celery salt
300 g (10½ oz) hot-smoked salmon

Preheat the oven to 220°C (430°F). Line a baking tray with baking paper.

Heat the oil in a small saucepan over a medium–high heat until it has a good quiver. Pat the capers dry with paper towel then add to the hot oil. Shake the pan occasionally and cook until they look puffed and crisp. Transfer the capers to a paper towel using a slotted spoon. Set the pan of oil aside.

Spread the potato gems on the baking tray. Pour over the caper oil and toss to coat. Bake until golden, around 20 minutes.

Meanwhile, zest the lemons then slice into wedges. Spread the sour cream on a serving platter and mix in the horseradish cream, most of the herbs, lemon zest and a spritz of lemon juice. Season with salt, be strong with the pepper.

Sprinkle some celery salt on top of the potato gems to taste. Toss to coat.

Top the sour cream spread with the gems and flake the smoked salmon over the top. Garnish with the remaining herbs and the fried capers. Serve with lemon wedges on the side. Forks are handy here, as are fingers (and pockets?).

✱ THE SUBS
  CAPERS pitted green olives
  SOUR CREAM cream cheese / Greek yoghurt
  HORSERADISH CREAM dijon mustard / wholegrain mustard
  CHIVES AND DILL parsley / mint / basil
  CELERY SALT chicken salt / garlic salt / sea salt flakes
  HOT-SMOKED SALMON smoked salmon / cooked salmon

RIVIERA PANCAKE

GF / NF

When you serve this, announce it with a big rolling 'R' and declare it 'faRrrrrinata'. It's a Ligurian chickpea pancake that, at its core, is a simple baked combination of besan (chickpea flour), water and oil. With different names in different Italian regions, the 'faRrrrrinata' morphs again when it moves to France and Gibraltar. But I'm sticking with the Ligurian version, because that's where I plan on making it again in my Riviera-side villa.

DRINK BICICLETTA
SNACKS 4-6
COMMITMENT GO THE DISTANCE

150 g (5½ oz) besan (chickpea flour)
125 ml (4 fl oz/½ cup) extra-virgin olive oil
bunch of sage, leaves picked
50 g (1¾ oz) grated parmesan,
   plus extra to serve
1 garlic clove, crushed or finely chopped
½ red onion, thinly sliced
100 g (3½ oz) mascarpone
zest and juice of 1 lemon
80 g (2¾ oz) anchovy fillets

Add the besan to a bowl with 300 ml (10 fl oz) water and whisk until smooth. Cover and leave to sit for at least 3 hours (overnight would be even better).

Preheat the oven to 220°C (430°F).

Add 80 ml (2½ fl oz/⅓ cup) of the oil and the sage leaves to a 20 × 25 cm (8 × 10 in) baking dish. Bake the sage until crisp, about 5 minutes. Move the leaves to a piece of paper towel and season with salt. Reserve the oil in the baking dish.

Use a spoon to gently skim (and discard) any foam on the surface of the chickpea batter, then whisk in the parmesan, garlic and leftover olive oil. Generously season with salt and pepper.

Now pour the batter into the baking dish with the sage oil and arrange the onion on top. Bake for 8 minutes, or until the top is just starting to set. Now turn the oven grill (broiler) to high and grill until lightly golden, about 4 minutes.

Meanwhile, combine the mascarpone with the lemon zest, a spritz of lemon juice and a hefty pinch of salt and pepper (especially pepper).

When the farinata is finito, make haste and serve warm. Slice into (any size) pieces and move to a board. Smoodge or dollop on some mascarpone, then top with sage leaves, anchovies and extra parmesan, or just make your people do it themselves. Crack over some more pepper. Serve with lemon wedges.

✱ THE SUBS
SAGE rosemary / thyme / basil
PARMESAN pecorino / cheddar / your hard cheese of choice
RED ONION brown onion / shallots / any onion type
MASCARPONE crème fraîche / sour cream / fresh mozzarella / burrata
ANCHOVY capers / olives

HOT CHIPS

Truffle cheese & rosemary

Bake with: grated truffle manchego, rosemary

Top with: chilli flakes

Dip into: garlic aioli

Five-spice & fried shallot

Bake with: Chinese five-spice, onion powder

Top with: fried shallots

Dip into: chilli mayo'

Garam masala & kasundi

Bake with: garam masala

Top with: lime zest, coriander (cilantro)

Dip into: yoghurt, tomato kasundi

Haloumi & oregano

Bake with: haloumi chunks, fennel, dried oregano

Top with: lemon zest

Dip into: mixed olive dip

Frozen hot chips, like many other formats of frozen potato, are a gift – a freezer gift. Bake them according to the packet instructions, but don't be afraid to bake longer for a better crunch. It's an eye job. Or, better yet, an air fryer job. Seriously.

As per, be generous with these toppings and don't forget to season very well.

LAX LOAF WITH THE LOT

SNACKS 8-10

NF / VEG

**Right, you're going to have to get off the couch
the night before you plan on presenting this
Picasso piece. I know, it feels like a push, but
don't worry – it's easy. We can all be talented
bakers when we make a no-knead bread.**

**I envisioned this recipe as a fusion of Turkish
bread, focaccia and lavosh. And that, it has
become. Serve with or without cheese-board-
esque sides, because it already comes filled
with half of them anyway.**

600 g (1 lb 5 oz) bread flour
7 g (¼ oz) dried yeast
500 ml (17 fl oz/2 cups) lukewarm water
100 g (3½ oz) hard cheese of your choice
2 tablespoons sesame seeds
1 tablespoon nigella seeds
2 teaspoons caraway seeds
1 tablespoon fine sea salt
125 ml (4 fl oz/½ cup) extra-virgin olive oil,
    plus extra for greasing and serving
80 ml (2½ fl oz/⅓ cup) sesame oil
150 g (5½ oz) pitted mixed olives
bunch of oregano, leaves picked

✱ THE SUBS
  NIGELLA SEEDS extra caraway seeds /
  black sesame seeds
  CARAWAY SEEDS fennel seeds / cumin seeds
  OREGANO rosemary / thyme

Combine the flour and yeast in a large bowl.
Add the water and give it a really good mix to
combine into a shaggy dough. Cover and stand
in a warm spot for 15 minutes to give the yeast
a chance to activate.

Meanwhile, cut the cheese into small chunks.
Combine the sesame seeds, nigella seeds,
caraway seeds and salt in a bowl.

Add the cheese to the dough with 1 tablespoon
of the olive oil, 1 tablespoon of the sesame
oil and half each of the seed mix, olives and
oregano. Mix with your hands (it feels nice) until
smooth. Cover and leave in the fridge overnight,
or for 8–12 hours.

Take a deep 20 × 25 cm (8 × 10 in) baking dish
and grease well with olive oil. Tip in the dough
and use your fingers to spread it to the edges.
Cover and leave for 2–3 hours in a warm spot
until doubled in size.

When it's looking almost there, heat the oven
to 220°C (430°F).

Now create dimples in the dough with your
fingers, then stud with the remaining olives
and oregano. Sprinkle over the remaining seed
mix. Drizzle over 60 ml (2 fl oz/¼ cup) of the
olive oil.

Bake for 25–30 minutes, or until golden
brown and hollow when tapped on the base.
Immediately drizzle over the remaining olive oil
and sesame oil. Let the bread cool for
5 minutes in the dish, then remove and cool
on a wire rack.

Slice and serve with more olive oil for dipping
and any extra sides you feel like.

TINI'S TINI

POURS 4

You've heard stranger things, but this drink is dedicated to a bird – my friend Paris's deceased tiny budgie, Tini. Named after our favourite filthy drink, this chatty, and actually chirpy, winged creature proved too precious for this planet.

Tini's mum Paris has a special skill. She can stir up a Tini (the drink) in any shape, form or mindset, with exquisite ass-shaking ease. This is for her, and her bird, so Tini can live on in our V-shaped glasses. If I could skewer all our olives with a feather stem in Tini's memory, I would, but that's a bit dark.

Not to mess too much with a good thing, but we're adding a little pickle to mix and stick. All I'm going to say is 'do it' because, quite frankly, I'm out of excuses for letting pickles creep their way into so many recipes. It's a bit uncouth, which makes it even better.

180 ml (6 fl oz) dry gin or vodka
60 ml (2 fl oz/¼ cup) dry vermouth
30 ml (1 fl oz) Sicilian olive brine
30 ml (1 fl oz) cornichon brine

TOPPERS
fat Sicilian olives
cornichons

Put your martini glasses in the freezer and leave to get well frosty and cold. About 20 minutes.

Skewer your toppers, if you have a pointy thing, or just plonk them in at the end.

Now, half-fill a jug or cocktail shaker with ice. Pour in all the liquids, and it's time to stir silly. You want the jug to become properly cold – this is about achieving maximum chill.

With a strainer or fine sieve, strain and divide the Tini mix between the chilled martini glasses.

Top with your skewered briny bites or just drop them in to fish out later.

'To Tini!'

THE SPICE AND SMOKE SHOW

Stoke the fire and feel the sizzle, because you're about to turn up the heat like the class act you are. Eating anything hot (say, nose-searing hot English mustard) seems like a bit of a sadistic ordeal. We avoid pain yet fearlessly squirt hot sauce over just about anything, and request wasabi when shovelling sushi. Why? The body digs that push and pull.

When you first ingest anything fiery, your body interprets it as a threat (no doubt). But like a primal hero, after your body realises it's okay, the brain releases endorphins (the feel-good ones). You're left with a hormone high, pumped by the fact that you're not actually dying.

Loving to torture ourselves, we've created and played with so many hot ingredients, many of which are here, including harissa, 'nduja, Tabasco, jalapeños, Calabrese salami and wasabi. There are smoky things too, because what would a fire be without a little smoke? There's a fair share of smoked seafood and, like the good Hungarian girl I am, a generous dose of paprika, too.

PSA: There's a spice challenge in here. It's exhilarating. If you're in pain and your endorphins aren't kicking in yet, reach for dairy, not water. Okay?

SPANISH SPUDS

DF / GF / NF

Anything Spanish (and Spanish adjacent) reminds me of Milli, my friend and culinary Yoda since I was nineteen.

Together we devoured our way through Malaga, and it's the combination of potatoes and octopus that bring it all back. Maybe not on par with sitting on a plastic chair on an Andalusian beach, but the sentiment is there, and it takes seconds.

Most microwave potatoes come with herbs and butter, and that's very welcome. Feel free to boil the potatoes instead if you have some lying around. It's cheaper too.

DRINK TINTO DE VERANO
SNACKS 6–8
COMMITMENT QUICKIE

400 g (14 oz) pre-cooked microwave
   baby potatoes
2 × 250 g (9 oz) tubs marinated octopus
   (150 g/5½ oz drained weight)
100 g (3½ oz) roasted capsicum
   (bell pepper) strips

TOPPERS
extra-virgin olive oil
pimentón (smoked Spanish paprika)
parsley

Microwave the potatoes according to the packet instructions then slice into quarters or rounds. Slice the octopus, if not sliced already.

Arrange the potatoes, octopus and capsicum strips on a plate. There's not much else to it, so you might as well be arty.

Give it all a proper good season with salt, a proper good drizzle with oil and a proper good dusting with pimentón, like proper. Tear over the parsley (be proper with that too, if you like).

Stab with skewers or forks to eat.

✱ THE SUBS
  MICROWAVE BABY POTATOES boiled baby potatoes
  PIMENTÓN smoked paprika / regular shelf paprika

AN EVENING WITH FRENCH MEN

NF

I'm glad we've established we're okay with beige food now, so I don't need to go making excuses for the colour of this.

This mackerel is a moment that channels our local French wine bar, which we are devoted to getting on a first-name basis with. Why? We just want the pâté on tap. Nothing at all to do with the French waiters.

DRINK KIR
SNACKS 4–6
COMMITMENT QUICKIE

100 g (3½ oz) smoked mackerel fillet
150 g (5½ oz) cream cheese
2 heaped tablespoons horseradish cream
2 tablespoons capers, drained, rinsed
  and chopped
small bunch of chives, snipped
zest and juice of 1 lemon

TOPPERS
extra-virgin olive oil
cornichons
pickled red onions

SCOOPERS
sliced baguette

Peel the skin off the mackerel (bin it) and flake the flesh into a serving bowl. Add the cream cheese, horseradish cream, capers, chives and lemon zest and juice. Mix to combine well. Give it a good season, especially with pepper. Drizzle some olive oil on top.

Spread the pâté over the bread. Eat with cornichons and pickled onions.

✳ THE SUBS
SMOKED MACKEREL hot-smoked salmon /
smoked trout / smoked barramundi
CREAM CHEESE crème fraîche / sour cream
CAPERS more cornichons
CHIVES dill / parsley
BAGUETTE bread of your choice

'NDUJA WITH SUPER HONEY

NF

It's so simple. You heat honey with a savoury element. This creates something similar to what my sister would describe as the uniqueness of a good date: a certain *'je ne sais quoi'* (she likes anything French).

Here, the savoury element is garlic, but you could try chilli (fresh or dried), spices (fennel, cumin or peppercorns), herbs (rosemary, thyme), or even just sea salt flakes (smoked sea salt would be wicked). You get it.

DRINK ITALICUS SPRITZ
SNACKS 4-6
COMMITMENT QUICKIE

3 garlic cloves
90 g (3 oz/¼ cup) honey
150 g (5½ oz) pickled hot peppers
150 g (5½ oz) 'nduja
100 g (3½ oz) asiago cheese

SCOOPERS
crusty bread

Bash the garlic or crush open with the side of a knife. Heat the honey and garlic in a small saucepan over a medium heat until properly frothing, about 1–2 minutes. Pour into a little serving bowl.

Tear the pickled peppers in half, unless you like it hot.

Arrange the peppers, 'nduja and cheese on a board. Leave the cheese shaving for the others to do – you've done enough – and serve with crusty bread and the bowl of honey on the side.

✱ **THE SUBS**
PICKLED HOT PEPPERS pickled jalapeños
'NDUJA cured or cooked chorizo / spicy salami
ASIAGO CHEESE pecorino / parmesan

RE-CALABRESE-ATING

NF

This may read like the antipasto section of the supermarket, and that's because it mostly is. Just slightly more curated. Go easy on yourself.

Taralli are yeasted Italian appetiser biscuits made with fennel, white wine and olive oil. I found them in that same section.

DRINK NEGRONI
SNACKS 4–6
COMMITMENT QUICKIE

80 g (2¾ oz) tapenade
250 g (9 oz) fresh mozzarella
120 g (4½ oz) cheese-stuffed cherry peppers
120 g (4½ oz) hot Calabrese salami

TOPPERS
basil leaves
garlic oil
taralli

Spread the tapenade over a serving platter. Tear over the mozzarella and cheese-stuffed peppers. Arrange the salami over and around.

Top with basil, a drizzle of garlic oil and a good crack of black pepper. Serve with taralli, making sure to swipe the salty tapenade base.

✱ THE SUBS
TAPENADE pesto of your choice
FRESH MOZZARELLA burrata / ricotta / provolone / feta
CHEESE-STUFFED CHERRY PEPPERS cheese-stuffed olives
HOT CALABRESE SALAMI any hot salami
TARALLI grissini or any Italian cracker

BEANBAG CHIPS

DF / GF / VEG / VEGAN

Chilli chips send me straight back to 6 pm on a school night, watching *The Simpsons*, nestled in a beanbag. But now with no antennae to battle (or commercials), there's time to add extra chilli, slice makrut lime leaves and stay up past my bedtime.

A serious note on seasoning: freshly cracked black pepper will always taste best, but if you're avoiding too much wrist action, go pre-cracked. Extra salting will depend on how salted the chips come – you'll have to taste them. Torture.

DRINK PICKLEBACK
SNACKS 2-4
COMMITMENT QUICKIE

1 tablespoon freshly cracked black pepper
½ teaspoon chilli powder
2 teaspoons onion powder
2 teaspoons garlic powder
165 g (6 oz) salted potato chips
100 g (3½ oz) salted peanuts
4 makrut lime leaves, thinly sliced
1 long red chilli, sliced
olive oil spray
2 limes

Preheat the oven to 220°C (430°F). Line a baking tray with baking paper.

Combine the pepper, and chilli, onion and garlic powders in a bowl.

Spread the chips, peanuts, lime leaves and chilli in the tray. Spray with some olive oil.

Sprinkle the spice mix over the top and give it all a good toss to coat. Bake until the chips are golden and shiny, about 5 minutes.

Grate the lime zest over the lot, taste and add a bit more salt if needed.

✱ THE SUBS
CHILLI POWDER chilli flakes
PEANUTS cashews
LONG RED CHILLI chilli flakes

A TOMATO'S PURPOSE

DF / NF

Imagine Spanish pan con tomate (bread with tomato), but with something a little extra. Not because it needs it, but because crispy chilli oil loves it.

If you're not already, it's time to start smelling the tomatoes you buy with the same gusto you test-squeeze avocados for ripeness. They should smell noticeably sweet and fragrantly … tomato. As you would expect.

Keep the drained tomato juice for the Bloody good Mary (page 95) and season the skins and add them to salads, sandwiches or mix back through this chilli-tomato dip.

DRINK CUCUMBER MINT GIMLET
SNACKS 4–6
COMMITMENT QUICKIE

700 g (1 lb 9 oz) ripe tomatoes,
    destemmed, halved
6 slices sourdough
extra-virgin olive oil, for drizzling,
    plus extra to serve
3 garlic cloves, peeled

TOPPERS
crispy chilli oil
black vinegar
fish sauce
toasted sesame seeds

Put a sieve over a bowl and grate the tomatoes with a box grater, starting from the cut side. Add the tomato pulp to the sieve to drain, and retain the skins and juice (see intro).

Now, heat a large frying pan over a medium–high heat. Generously drizzle one side of the bread slices with olive oil (you'll do the other side in a bit). Fry the bread oiled-side down in the pan until golden, about 2 minutes. Drizzle the other side with oil, flip and fry for another 2 minutes until golden. (You may need to fry the bread in batches.)

Rub the garlic all over the fried bread, letting the coarse edges of the bread catch on the garlic.

Spread the tomato pulp on a serving plate. Season with salt and top with chilli oil and a dash of black vinegar and fish sauce, and a final drizzle of olive oil. Sprinkle over the sesame seeds.

Smell, scoop and spread the tomato mix over the fried bread.

* THE SUBS
    SOURDOUGH bread of your choice
    BLACK VINEGAR balsamic vinegar / rice vinegar /
    white-wine vinegar
    FISH SAUCE soy sauce / anchovies

BELLA MORTADELLA

NF

The jury is divided and I need you to weigh in: do you prefer your sandwich bread toasted or fresh? I can't make this decision for you. But I can offer you reasoning:

Toasted: You get some crunch, structural integrity and even the chance to fry your bread.

vs

Fresh: You get a soft and spongy texture (also a brilliant bite 'shock absorber') for maximum flavour absorption.

DRINK SPARKLING RED
SNACKS 10-12
COMMITMENT MINOR INVESTMENT

200 g (7 oz) pitted green olives
200 g (7 oz) marinated artichokes
80 ml (2½ fl oz/⅓ cup) extra-virgin olive oil
1 tablespoon fennel seeds
2 long red chillies, sliced
2 garlic cloves, chopped
bunch of fresh oregano, torn
350 g (12½ oz) ciabatta loaf
250 g (9 oz) mortadella
100 g (3½ oz) pre-sliced provolone
300 g (10½ oz) jar roasted peppers
300 g (10½ oz) burrata, sliced

TOPPERS
rocket (arugula)
parsley leaves
basil leaves

Smash the olives and artichokes by the easiest means (with a mortar and pestle; roughly chop with a knife; power scrunch with your hands – easier than it sounds).

Heat the oil, fennel seeds, chilli, garlic and oregano in a frying pan over a medium–high heat until fragrant and the oregano and chilli are starting to crisp, about 2–3 minutes. Take off the heat and season a little.

Slice the ciabatta in half lengthways, then open like a book. Spread the olive-artichoke smash over each side of the bread. Now layer the mortadella, provolone, peppers and burrata on top as you feel: alternate, do a little bit of each, then go back for more. Up to you.

Top with rocket and herbs. Spoon over the chilli-fennel oil and slice into bite-sized pieces. Bliss.

✱ THE SUBS
FENNEL SEEDS caraway seeds / anise seeds / cumin seeds
OREGANO rosemary / thyme
CIABATTA bread of your choice
PROVOLONE fontina / mozzarella / gouda / havarti / Comté
BURRATA mozzarella / bocconcini

MUSSELS THAT LIFT

GF / NF

DRINK RIOJA
SNACKS 4-6
COMMITMENT MINOR INVESTMENT

1 tablespoon extra-virgin olive oil
1 small red onion, sliced
250 g (9 oz) chorizo, sliced
3 garlic cloves, chopped
small bunch of parsley, chopped
drizzle of sherry vinegar
200 g (7 oz) goat's curd
100 g (3½ oz) Greek yoghurt
2 × 80 g (2¾ oz) tins smoked mussels
(no need to drain – the oil is good!)

SCOOPERS
salt and vinegar potato chips (crisps)

Let the record state: I do not like salt and vinegar chips. But, after drizzling extra sherry vinegar on these mussels, I can now see vinegar's big value here. To be clear, I still voted for plain salted chips, so feel free to go for them too. Chilli chips would also be nice.

Heat the oil in a large frying pan over a high heat. Cook the onion, chorizo and garlic for about 8 minutes, or until golden brown. Remove from the heat and toss through the parsley and sherry vinegar. Season and leave to cool a little.

Mix the goat's curd and yoghurt together on a serving plate, give it a good season and spread it out a bit. Top with the chorizo mix.

Crack open the mussels and chips. Stack the mussels and chorizo, scoop the dip, then layer on a chip.

✱ THE SUBS
RED ONION any onion
PARSLEY basil
GOAT'S CURD goat's cheese
SALT AND VINEGAR POTATO CHIPS chips of your choice

BREADSTICKS WITH HARISSA TOUM

DF / VEG / VEGAN

DRINK DRY ROSÉ
SNACKS 4-6
COMMITMENT MINOR INVESTMENT

1 × 500 g (1 lb 2 oz) small loaf olive bread
60 ml (2 fl oz/¼ cup) garlic oil
bunch of marjoram
200 g (7 oz) baba ghanoush
   (store-bought is good)
200 g (7 oz) toum (Lebanese garlic dip)
2 tablespoons harissa

TOPPERS
drizzle of extra-virgin olive oil
toasted pine nuts

I strongly disagree with the negative sentiment attached to the garlic aroma (the breathy kind). In protest, I'm serving double the garlic: toum (Lebanese garlic sauce) and crispy garlic-oiled breadsticks. So there.

Compared to the breadsticks you're imagining, this version is, in fact, a bread loaf sliced into sticks.

Heat the oven to 220°C (430°F). Line a baking tray with baking paper.

Slice the bread into thin-ish sticks then lay on the tray. Drizzle the garlic oil on top, then tear over the marjoram (reserve a few sprigs to garnish), give it a good season, then toss and rub to coat. Bake until golden and crisp, about 15–20 minutes, turning the bread over halfway through. Remove from the oven and leave to cool.

Add the baba ghanoush and toum to a serving plate. Season and vaguely stir to combine.

Top with the harissa and give it a little swirl. Drizzle with the olive oil, then sprinkle the pine nuts and reserved marjoram on top. Grind a little more black pepper over that.

Scoop with the very realistic breadsticks.

✱ THE SUBS
  OLIVE BREAD any good crusty loaf
  GARLIC OIL extra-virgin olive oil
  MARJORAM thyme / oregano
  PINE NUTS pistachio nuts / almonds / seeds / hazelnuts

WASABI PEA DIP

DF / GF / VEG / VEGAN

DRINK SAKE
SNACKS 6–8
COMMITMENT MINOR INVESTMENT

200 g (7 oz) frozen peas
zest and juice of 2 limes
3 cm (1¼ in) piece ginger, peeled and grated
bunch of coriander (cilantro), leaves picked
2 tablespoons wasabi paste
2 tablespoons white miso paste
1 tablespoon tahini
1 tablespoon sesame oil

TOPPERS
wasabi peas
tamari almonds

SCOOPERS
puffed seaweed chips

Straw that broke the camel's back? Dip that broke the blender. But like, in a positive way. I mean, what an honour. (This won't happen to yours, ours was hanging on by a thread.)

The puffed seaweed chips are a nice touch, but no stress if you can't locate them; any seaweed-style cracker, or any cracker for that matter, will do.

Bring a kettle of water to the boil. Tip the peas into a heatproof bowl and pour enough boiled water over the peas to cover them. Set aside to defrost, only about 1 minute, then drain.

To a food processor, blender, or whatever blitzer you've got, add the defrosted peas, lime zest and juice, ginger, coriander (save some leaves to garnish, if you want), wasabi, miso, tahini, sesame oil and 60 ml (2 fl oz/¼ cup) water. Blitz to a smooth puree. Adjust the seasoning – trust your palate.

Scoop the dip into a bowl. Top with the wasabi peas and tamari almonds. Garnish with coriander, if you saved some. Eat with your seaweed-y scooper.

✱ THE SUBS
FROZEN PEAS frozen edamame
WHITE MISO PASTE soy sauce

EXTRA OLD ELOTE

GF / NF

DRINK CHELADA
SNACKS 4-6
COMMITMENT MINOR INVESTMENT

410 g (14½ oz) tin corn kernels, drained
800 g (1 lb 12 oz) tin tomatillos, drained
100 g (3½ oz) mayo'
100 g (3½ oz) sour cream
100 g (3½ oz) feta, crumbled
½ red onion, finely chopped
bunch of coriander (cilantro), leaves picked,
    finely chopped
zest and juice of 1 lime
100 g (3½ oz) cheddar, grated

TOPPERS
XO sauce

SCOOPERS
corn chips (purple ones look cool)

Trade your hugs and kisses for another XO – the sauce. It's a spicy, salty condiment from Hong Kong made from a mix of dried seafood, spices and chilli. The XO means '*extra old*' as a way to emphasise the prestige of this punchy sauce.

Try topping your eggs off with *extra old* too.

Heat a large dry frying pan over a high heat. Char the corn in the hot pan for 5–8 minutes, tossing occasionally. The corn may pop about, that's normal, just cover with a colander if it bothers you, then take off the heat to cool.

Roughly tear the tomatillos into a colander or sieve and leave to keep draining.

In a dipping bowl, combine the mayo', sour cream, crumbled feta, onion, coriander, lime zest and cheddar, then add the charred corn and tomatillos. Give it all a good season and add lime juice to taste.

Spoon over the XO sauce – as much as you want. Scoop up with corn chips.

✱ THE SUBS
    SOUR CREAM cream cheese / crème fraîche
    LIME lemon
    XO SAUCE chilli oil of your choice

LATE-NIGHT NOODS

VEG

A bleary-eyed cup-o-noodles at 3 am is my jam. Best enjoyed sitting on a kerb outside the petrol station I bought them from. I'm not missing the couch. This time though, I'm eager to *start* my night with them. I can always bookend it too.

DRINK WHISKY HIGHBALL
SNACKS 6-8
COMMITMENT MINOR INVESTMENT

2 × 120 g (4½ oz) instant noodle packets
   (I use Shin Ramyun)
50 g (1¾ oz) seaweed rice crackers
100 g (3½ oz) cashews
1 tablespoon honey
2 tablespoons vegetable oil
100 g (3½ oz) wasabi peas
2 × 5 g (⅛ oz) packets seaweed snacks

TOPPERS
wasabi mayo' (optional)

Heat the oven to 220°C (430°F). Line a baking tray with baking paper.

With your hands, crack and crunch the dried noodles and rice crackers over the tray. Add the cashews, too.

Combine the noodle spice mix, honey and oil in a little bowl. Add 1 tablespoon water to loosen and give it a good stir – add a little more honey if it's too hot for you. Pour over the noodle mix then toss and massage in with your hands.

Bake until golden, tossing halfway, about 6–8 minutes. Leave to cool completely to crisp.

Sprinkle over the veg' flakes (if your packet noodles came with any) and wasabi peas. Crackle and crunch over the seaweed snacks, then toss everything together.

Drizzle over some wasabi mayo' if you want.

✱ THE SUBS
SEAWEED RICE CRACKERS rice cracker
of your choice
CASHEWS peanuts / tamari almonds

JUICY JALAPS

GF / NF / VEG

My head says the heat is mild, but my heart says the Greek yoghurt and sour cream coolers are necessary. You decide.

This is also a place for a side of guacamole. No recipe needed, because we all have someone who makes 'the best guacamole'. Also, if you take your corn chips cheese-flavoured, this is the moment for them too.

DRINK MARGARITA
SNACKS 4-6
COMMITMENT MINOR INVESTMENT

10 jalapeños
2 tablespoons extra-virgin olive oil
100 g (3½) sour cream
100 g (3½) Greek yoghurt
1 lime, zested and cut into wedges
2 garlic cloves, grated or finely chopped
small bunch of coriander (cilantro),
    leaves and stems chopped
150 g (5½ oz) smoked cheddar, grated
2 tablespoons chipotle sauce

SCOOPERS
corn chips

TOPPERS
guacamole (optional)

Preheat the oven grill (broiler) to high. Line a baking tray with foil.

Halve the jalapeños lengthways and scoop out the seeds. Season, drizzle the oil over the jalapeños and rub to coat. Grill, skin side up, until starting to char, about 8 minutes.

Combine the sour cream, yoghurt, lime zest, a good squeeze of lime juice, the garlic and all the coriander in a bowl. Season well to taste.

Now, turn over the par-grilled jalapeños and sprinkle the cheese on top with the intention of mostly filling them. Grill again until melted and golden brown, about 5 minutes.

Swirl the chipotle through the sour cream dip. Scoop with corn chips, then top with a jalapeño with an optional side of guacamole.

✱ THE SUBS
SOUR CREAM cream cheese / crème fraîche / more Greek yoghurt
LIME lemon
SMOKED CHEDDAR regular cheddar / gouda / mozzarella / melty cheese of your choice
CHIPOTLE SAUCE sriracha with a pat of smoked paprika

STICKY NUGGIES

NF

Hi, yeah, can I please have a twelve-pack of nuggets, a medium fries and a vanilla thickshake? Oh, and coat the nuggets in a hot hoisin sauce, top with toasted sesame seeds, spring onions and go strong on the sriracha, please.

If you're like my sister, you'd swap grating garlic and ginger for the pre-prepped supermarket version. She's the gold standard of lazy. Or efficient – however you want to read it.

DRINK DARK & STORMY
SNACKS 4–6
COMMITMENT MINOR INVESTMENT

1 kg (2 lb 3 oz) frozen chicken nuggets
100 g (3½ oz) honey
200 ml (7 fl oz) hoisin
2 tablespoons sriracha, plus extra to serve
4 cm (1½ in) piece ginger, peeled and
    finely grated
3 garlic cloves, finely grated
zest and juice of 1 lime

TOPPERS
toasted sesame seeds
sliced spring onion (scallion)
kewpie mayo'

Preheat the oven to 220°C (430°F). Line a baking tray with foil and spread the nuggets out on the tray. Bake until golden, about 18–20 minutes, turning halfway.

Add the remaining ingredients to a small saucepan and bring to the boil over a high heat. Reduce the heat to medium–high and simmer until reduced and sticky, about 4–6 minutes.

Tip the nuggets onto a serving platter or leave on the tray. Pour the sauce over the nuggets and toss to coat. Top with the sesame seeds and spring onion and serve with kewpie and extra sriracha.

* THE SUBS
  SRIRACHA sambal oelek / hot sauce of your choice
  SESAME SEEDS crushed peanuts / cashews
  SPRING ONION coriander (cilantro)
  KEWPIE MAYO' regular mayo'

IT'S A WING THING

NF

Would you use knives and forks with a pizza? A burger? A hot dog? No. Cutlery is futile here, too. If there's any time for sticky fingers, this is it. Submit to the stick and lick.

DRINK RUM ON THE ROCKS
SNACKS 4-6
COMMITMENT GO THE DISTANCE

35 g (1¼ oz) cornflour (cornstarch)
2 tablespoons smoked salt
2 tablespoons barbecue spice mix
2 tablespoons smoked paprika
1.5 kg (3 lb 5 oz) chicken wings
olive oil spray
600 ml (20½ fl oz) Coke
125 ml (4 fl oz/½ cup) sriracha
250 ml (8½ fl oz/1 cup) smoky barbecue sauce
60 ml (2 fl oz/¼ cup) Worcestershire sauce
2 tablespoons brown sugar

TOPPERS
sour cream

Preheat the oven to 220°C (430°F). Line a baking tray with baking paper and top with a wire rack.

Combine the cornflour, smoked salt, barbecue spice mix, smoked paprika and a really good crack of black pepper in a large mixing bowl.

Add the wings and toss really well to coat. Spread out on the wire rack, skin side up. Give them a little spray with the oil. Bake for about 35 minutes or until cooked through.

Combine the Coke, sriracha, barbecue sauce, Worcestershire sauce and brown sugar in a saucepan. Bring to the boil over a high heat, then reduce the heat to medium–high and simmer until well reduced and sticky, about 20–25 minutes. Let cool.

Tip the wings onto a serving plate. Pour over the Coke sauce and toss to coat. Dollop on some sour cream.

✱ THE SUBS
BARBECUE SPICE MIX / SMOKED PAPRIKA
extra of either
SRIRACHA hot sauce of your choice
SMOKY BARBECUE SAUCE tomato sauce

DIPPING OILS

Fresh tomato & oregano

diced tomato

oregano leaves

torn basil

grated parmesan

balsamic vinegar

chilli paste

Paprika & anchovy

torn anchovy fillets

smoked paprika

thinly sliced garlic

torn parsley

sherry vinegar

torn green olives

Togarashi & ponzu

togarashi

sesame oil

soy sauce

ponzu

thinly sliced spring onion (scallion)

grated ginger

toasted sesame seeds

Aleppo pepper & walnut

Aleppo pepper

pomegranate molasses

lemon zest and juice

chilli flakes

crushed roasted walnuts

torn mint

Start with a generous pour of good-quality olive oil (extra-virgin would be best) then top and tear over the rest and don't forget to season. Pass the bread.

THE RING OF FIRE

SNACKS 6–8

NF

This spicy challenge doesn't involve chilli. This game of risk only needs a die (that's dice, singular), any bottle and an openness to potentially eat a large spoonful of hot English mustard. The condiment momentarily abuses your nostrils and forces your eyes shut as you digest the (addictive) sharp and pungent pangs, then rapidly leaves, giving you the bold (ignorant) confidence to roll the die again. And again.

To be clear, this is the only time you will stack and skewer in this book. And it's for good reason; you're building something somewhat menacing.

100 g (3½ oz) sweet mustard pickle
1 tablespoon dijon mustard
500 g (1 lb 2 oz) jar dill pickles
250 g (9 oz) shaved leg ham
50 g (1¾ oz) hot English mustard

TOPPERS
skewers
crackers
cheddar cheese, sliced

Stack it:

Combine the sweet mustard pickle and dijon mustard in a bowl. Drain the pickles and slice into bite-sized pieces (I enjoy a pickle wedge, personally).

Divide the ham into (at least) twenty-five portions. Swipe the sweet dijon mustard mix over twenty of the ham portions. Spoon hot English mustard over the remaining five (be as generous/brazen as you wish). Top each with a pickle. Wrap the ham around the filling, skewer and plonk on a cracker.

Play it:

Arrange the ham stacks in a circle with a bottle in the centre (a tabasco one feels oddly relevant). Have cheddar chasers ready in the wings.

Going around in a circle – left to right seems to be the way – take turns rolling the die. This is where the tension builds. Whenever someone rolls a one, that person must spin the bottle and eat whichever ham stack it lands on – in one whole mouthful. Chase with cheddar, if you need.

I've seen people with watering eyes demand spit plates, but that's up to you.

BLOODY GOOD MARY

POURS 4

With a bolstering whack of wasabi, the tender touch of Tabasco and a good knock of ginger, Mary is the master of mornings. Or evenings. Or whenever. How bloody good.

30 g (1 oz) wasabi paste
2 tablespoons Tabasco
2 tablespoons Worcestershire sauce
1 tablespoon fish sauce
350 ml (12 fl oz) vodka
700 ml (23½ fl oz) tomato juice
40 ml (1¼ fl oz) ginger cordial
50 g (1¾ oz) ginger, peeled and crushed or sliced
2 limes, halved

TOPPERS
salt flakes
chilli flakes
toasted sesame seeds
celery stalks

In a small bowl, combine the wasabi, Tabasco, Worcestershire and fish sauce.

To a large jug, add the vodka, tomato juice, cordial, wasabi mix and ginger. Squeeze in the lime juice and add the rinds to the jug too. Stir to combine and balance the flavour by splashing in juice, cordial or Tabasco as needed.

Combine a big pinch of salt flakes, chilli flakes and sesame seeds on a flat plate. Wet the rims of four glasses and roll in the salt mix. Add ice to the glasses and pour over the Mary mix. Add celery stalks to each glass and be on your way.

✳ THE SUBS
 TABASCO hot sauce of your choice
 FISH SAUCE soy sauce

HOW GOOD IS ACID?

Hunt down your local lemon trees and pile up on the citrus – this is about to get juicy. Acid is a sharp-witted star. With a personality that hits you in the same way it hits your palate, acid demands attention. It's direct: has a bit of cheek and leaves you salivating. Know someone like that?

It's easy to get your fix, as there's an entire family tree of citrus to pick from and an A–Z of vinegars. Not forgetting the briny bits (cornichons, capers or pickled veg'), tangy yoghurts, or just about anything that makes your cells feel like they're doing the Riverdance. We'll also be big on bright herbs here, seafood and anything else that makes you feel 'fresh to death'.

I know you'd never let a good thing go to waste. So, keep any remaining halves, cheeks, quarters and wedges and squeeze the juice into ice-cube trays. Or just straight-up freeze the citrus pieces themselves and throw them into a drink for an instant zesty edge. So chill!

Side note: if you've located a neighbourhood tree and it's missing the actual citrus, still pick the leaves. Crush them with your hands, have a whiff and use in soups, curries and beyond.

NUTTY WATERMELON

DF / GF

Not just a juicy arm-dripping beach snack, watermelon absorbs flavour like our skin absorbs sunscreen. Pouring this tamarind dressing over the watermelon slices turns the fruit into a triangular trifecta of flavour (sweet-salty-tangy). Add the toppers just before serving to keep them crunchy.

DRINK LEMONGRASS MOJITO
SNACKS 4–6
COMMITMENT QUICKIE

zest and juice of 1 lime
2 tablespoons tamarind paste
2 tablespoons fish sauce
2 tablespoons brown sugar
1 tablespoon neutral oil,
   like vegetable or sunflower
1 tablespoon hot water
1 long red chilli
¼ watermelon

TOPPERS
fried shallots
chopped salted beer nuts
Thai basil leaves

In a bowl, combine the lime zest and juice, tamarind paste, fish sauce, brown sugar, oil and hot water. Taste and season.

Thinly slice the chilli and cut the watermelon into wedges.

Sort of splay and arrange the watermelon on a platter. Spoon over the dressing. Top with the fried shallots, nuts and Thai basil.

✱ THE SUBS
TAMARIND PASTE combine ½ tablespoon rice-wine vinegar and ½ tablespoon brown sugar
CHOPPED BEER NUTS roasted cashews
THAI BASIL coriander (cilantro) / mint

RILLETTES AND PICKLED GRAPES

DF / NF

DRINK PINOT NOIR
SNACKS 4–6
COMMITMENT QUICKIE

250 ml (8½ fl oz/1 cup) apple-cider vinegar
pinch of whole black peppercorns (optional)
2 bay leaves (optional)
2 tablespoons caster (superfine) sugar
1 tablespoon salt
300 g (10½ oz) black seedless grapes
bunch of tarragon, leaves picked
180 g (6½ oz) duck rillettes

SCOOPERS
rye crackers

TOPPERS
cornichons

I do urge you to pickle grapes. They may seem plump already, but there's still plenty of flavour-absorbing scope, I swear. Store leftovers (if any) in a jar to serve with cheese or more meats.

I'm also wondering if you like tarragon? It's quite like liquorice, which I don't like, but I do like tarragon. Go figure. With notes of citrus and sweet spice, it's different to the lolly you may be imagining. If you're still not convinced, I refuse to force feed you. Try rosemary, thyme, oregano or even basil instead.

To a small saucepan, add the vinegar, 250 ml (8½ fl oz/1 cup) water, peppercorns and bay leaves, if using, and the sugar and salt. Bring to the boil over a medium heat.

Add the grapes and tarragon (save a few leaves for garnish), then cover and remove from the heat. Set aside until cooled completely.

Crack open the rillettes with a utensil at its side. Munch rillettes atop crackers with pickled grapes and, as always, cornichons, faithfully.

✱ THE SUBS
APPLE-CIDER VINEGAR white-wine vinegar /
red-wine vinegar
BLACK SEEDLESS GRAPES any variety of
seedless grapes
TARRAGON rosemary / thyme / oregano / basil
DUCK RILLETTES pork rillettes / pâté of your choice
RYE CRACKERS cracker of your choice

SALMON ROTI

NF

This recipe was originally destined for pre-made crêpes, but the supermarket didn't agree. What it offered instead was roti, and it really knew best. Flaky, willingly torn and with layers that love being fried in butter, now we do exactly that.

Add eggs to call it brunch.

DRINK BELLINI
SNACKS 4-6
COMMITMENT QUICKIE

250 g (9 oz) cream cheese
bunch of dill, chopped
1 lemon, zested and cut into wedges
1 tablespoon wholegrain mustard
butter, for frying
300 g (10½ oz) roti
500 g (1 lb 2 oz) smoked salmon

TOPPERS
pickled onions
carton of cress

Spoon the cream cheese into a serving bowl (or leave it in the tub) and add half the dill, the lemon zest and mustard. Moosh to combine, then season.

Melt some butter in a large frying pan and, working in batches, fry the roti, tearing it if it doesn't fit the pan. If you're less inclined to pan-fry, heat the roti in the microwave or oven.

Arrange the salmon, roti, pickled onions and cress on a board or platter, whichever. With the special cream cheese on the side, tear the roti then spread and fill with the all sorts.

✱ THE SUBS
CREAM CHEESE sour cream / Greek yoghurt / mascarpone / crème fraîche / goat's cheese
DILL chives / parsley / mint
WHOLEGRAIN MUSTARD dijon mustard / hot English mustard
PICKLED ONIONS capers / cornichons / gherkins / any pickled veg'
CRESS watercress

TOONA SASHIMI

GF / NF

DRINK YUZUSHU
SNACKS 4–6
COMMITMENT QUICKIE

75 g (2¾ oz) wasabi kewpie mayo'
1 tablespoon mirin
2 tablespoons rice-wine vinegar
200 g (7 oz) sliced sashimi-grade tuna

TOPPERS
sliced Lebanese (short) cucumber
pickled ginger
sesame oil
nori furikake
fried shallots

SCOOPERS
shiso leaves (perilla leaves)

DIPPERS
soy sauce

Get sashimi-grade tuna, freshly sliced by the fishmongers. Forget butchering any silky hunk of tuna yourself and leave it to the sharp blades and slick moves of the masters.

If you find shiso, I'm celebrating! This fragrant leaf gives the combined fresh and floral essence of coriander, basil and mint, but with an extra spiciness. I pick mine from the sidewalk, but I'm sure good greengrocers will sort you out.

Arrange the cucumber, pickled ginger and shiso on a serving plate. Make it look nice.

On another serving plate, combine the wasabi mayo', mirin and rice-wine vinegar. Spread it out, then lay the tuna on top.

Drizzle some sesame oil over the tuna. Dust with the nori furikake, then top with the fried shallots. Pour some soy sauce into a little bowl.

Use the shiso, or any utensils, to bundle up the tuna, mayo' mix, cucumber and pickled ginger. Dip in the soy too, if you want.

✱ THE SUBS
WASABI KEWPIE MAYO' mix mayo' with wasabi paste to taste
MIRIN add 1 tablespoon more rice-wine vinegar with a pinch of caster (superfine) sugar
TUNA sashimi-grade fish of your choice
NORI FURIKAKE nori flakes / togarashi / crushed seaweed snack
SHISO LEAVES basil / coriander (cilantro)

POSTER PRAWNS

DF / GF / NF

Make the prawn work for you. Use pre-cooked if that's easier, go full entertainer on the barbecue, or just grill in the oven as below. Feeding less? Just halve the recipe. How breezy.

DRINK GIN & TONIC
SNACKS 8–12
COMMITMENT MINOR INVESTMENT

900 g (2 lb) peeled prawns (shrimp), tail on
4 garlic cloves, chopped
60 ml (2 fl oz/¼ cup) extra-virgin olive oil
250 g (9 oz/1 cup) mayo'
2 tablespoons dijon mustard
zest and juice of 1 lemon
100 g (3½ oz) baby capers, drained, rinsed
    and chopped
180 g (6½ oz) cornichons, chopped
bunch of dill, chopped

SCOOPERS
1 large bag crinkle-cut salted potato chips

Turn the oven grill (broiler) to high. Toss the prawns, garlic and oil on a baking tray, then season well.

Grill the prawns until cooked through, 8–10 minutes, charring is welcome.

Now to a serving plate, add the mayo', dijon, lemon zest and juice, capers, cornichons and half the dill. Smoosh around to combine, then taste and adjust the seasoning.

Arrange the prawns on top of the dip and sprinkle over the remaining dill.

Scoop the prawns, and layer as you wish with chips.

✱ THE SUBS
  DIJON MUSTARD wholegrain mustard /
  hot English mustard
  CORNICHONS gherkins / any sort of pickles
  DILL parsley, mint, tarragon (mix and match)
  CRINKLE-CUT CHIPS I'll leave the texture to you

CAULI & COMTÉ

GF / NF / VEG

We're pickling the cauliflower here and it's no big deal. You're merely heating a vinegar combo, pouring it over the cauliflower, then totting off to bed (because you're making this the night before). If time doesn't allow, anywhere from four-ish hours ahead would do.

Make the pickling a big deal though when the others appear, call the cheese shaving 'interactive' and put your feet up. Or have another sleep. You work so hard.

DRINK PÉT NAT
SNACKS 6–8
COMMITMENT MINOR INVESTMENT

½ cauliflower
250 ml (8½ fl oz/1 cup) apple-cider vinegar
250 ml (8½ fl oz/1 cup) white vinegar
55 g (2 oz/¼ cup) caster (superfine) sugar
2 tablespoons salt
2 teaspoons ground turmeric
2 heaped tablespoons horseradish cream
70 g (2½ oz) mayo'
100 g (3½ oz) Comté

TOPPERS
watercress

SCOOPERS
seed crackers

Cut the cauliflower into florets, including any leaves and stems. Add it all to a jar or bowl.

Add the vinegars, sugar, salt and turmeric to a small saucepan and heat over a medium heat. Give it a little stir until the sugar and salt have dissolved, about 4 minutes. Pour the vinegar mix straight over the cauliflower. Leave to cool, then cover and refrigerate until ready to serve.

Ready now? Combine the horseradish cream and mayo' in a bowl. Drain the cauliflower.

Assemble the cauliflower, Comté (with a slicer), watercress, crackers and horseradish mayo' however you feel. Try and eat it all in one mouthful. Do it.

✱ THE SUBS
APPLE-CIDER VINEGAR / WHITE VINEGAR
white-wine vinegar
COMTÉ gruyere / Swiss cheese / cheddar / fontina
WATERCRESS rocket (arugula)

LATE-FAST FATTEH

VEG

Eggs for dinner. Pancakes for dinner. Is that *brinner* or some other forced word fusion? Let's rename it, that name sucks. How about … late-fast? Or break-late? Or just nothing, because food doesn't demand any time of day, just a mouth, maybe teeth and a stomach.

Anyway, this is based on a Levantine dish called fatteh, usually eaten for breakfast, but in the name of snacks and a general gratitude for multiple crunchy elements (here it's pita and chickpeas), make whenever you want to eat it. Like, right now.

DRINK PALOMA
SNACKS 4–6
COMMITMENT MINOR INVESTMENT

300 g (10½ oz) heirloom cherry tomatoes, halved
½ fennel bulb, thinly sliced, fronds reserved
1 teaspoon sumac, plus extra for dusting
40 g (1½ oz) barberries
60 ml (2 fl oz/¼ cup) white-wine vinegar
60 ml (2 fl oz/¼ cup) extra-virgin olive oil, plus extra for roasting
2 large Lebanese flatbreads
400 g (14 oz) tin chickpeas, drained
60 g (2 oz/½ cup) slivered almonds
300 g (10½ oz) Greek yoghurt
60 g (2 oz) tahini
2 garlic cloves, grated or finely chopped

TOPPERS
mint

Preheat the oven to 220°C (430°F). Line two baking trays with baking paper.

Combine the tomatoes, fennel, sumac, barberries, white-wine vinegar and olive oil in a bowl. Season well then set aside to marinate.

Cut the flatbreads into strips, or whichever scooping shape you like. Pat the chickpeas dry with paper towel.

Lay the flatbread on one of the baking trays and spread the chickpeas and almonds out on the other. Give both the flatbreads and chickpeas a really good drizzle with olive oil and season. Toss to coat. Spread it all out again.

Bake the flatbread and chickpeas until both are golden and crisp. The flatbreads will be about 10 minutes, the chickpeas about 15 minutes.

Meanwhile, spoon the yoghurt and tahini onto a large platter. Add the garlic, give it a good season and spread the mixture over the platter.

Top with the marinated veg' and the roasted chickpea mix. Tear over the mint and reserved fennel fronds. Scoop with the toasted flatbreads.

✱ THE SUBS
HEIRLOOM CHERRY TOMATOES regular cherry tomatoes
FENNEL BULB celery / radishes / extra cherry tomatoes
BARBERRIES goji berries / cranberries / currants
LEBANESE FLATBREADS pita bread / flatbread of your choice
SLIVERED ALMONDS pine nuts / pistachio nuts / walnuts / almonds
GARLIC CLOVES large dollop of toum / drizzle of garlic oil

FRIED DOLMADES

GF / VEG

My friend Sush and I have tried our fair share of dolmades and reviewed accordingly. The biggest points are for firmness (please don't be too squishy or disintegrate at my touch), briny tang, rice chew and dill ratio. No dill is a dill-breaker. But you be the judge. Conduct your own dolmades research.

DRINK METAXA AND LEMON ON THE ROCKS
SNACKS 4–6
COMMITMENT MINOR INVESTMENT

150 g (5½ oz) Greek yoghurt
2 garlic cloves, finely chopped
1 lemon, zested and cut into wedges
180 g (6½ oz) feta
bunch of dill, chopped
500 g (1 lb 2 oz) dolmades
2 tablespoons extra-virgin olive oil,
    plus extra for drizzling

TOPPERS
pomegranate molasses
toasted slivered almonds

Add the yoghurt, garlic, lemon zest and a splash of water to a bowl. Crumble in the feta. Using an electric mixer, beat the yoghurt-feta mix until fluffy (if you can't be bothered, pulverise and mix with a spoon or fork instead, the taste won't change).

Add most of the dill and mix until well combined. Give it a good season, especially with pepper, then spread over a serving plate.

Pat the dolmades dry with paper towel (this will help them crisp up).

Heat the oil in a large frying pan over a medium–high heat. Fry the dolmades until golden, gently turning every now and then, 4–6 minutes.

Arrange the dolmades over the whipped feta. Drizzle with the pomegranate molasses and some extra olive oil. Sprinkle the slivered almonds and remaining dill on top. Serve with the lemon wedges on the side. Fingers engaged. Ready to go.

✱ THE SUBS
   DILL mint / parsley / basil / chives
   (or a combination of)
   POMEGRANATE MOLASSES balsamic glaze / honey
   SLIVERED ALMONDS any shape of almond /
   pine nuts / pistachio nuts / walnuts

FALAFELS, ETC.

VEG

This tahini sauce is a type of Lebanese dip called tarator. There are plenty of variations, some are blitzed with nuts like almonds and walnuts, others are just tahini, lemon, garlic and water. Leave out the Greek yoghurt if vegans come knocking.

DRINK CAIPIROSKA
SNACKS 4–6
COMMITMENT MINOR INVESTMENT

2 Lebanese (short) cucumbers
100 g (3½ oz) tahini
80 ml (2½ fl oz/⅓ cup) toum
2 tablespoons Greek yoghurt
½ bunch of coriander (cilantro), stems and leaves chopped separately
1 lemon, zested and cut into wedges
extra-virgin olive oil, for frying, dressing and drizzling
300 g (10½ oz) falafels, torn in half
2 tablespoons pistachio dukkah, plus extra for dusting
60 ml (2 fl oz/¼ cup) white-wine vinegar
200 g (7 oz) beetroot (beet) hummus

TOPPERS
Aleppo pepper

SCOOPERS
pita breads

Bash the cucumbers (a rolling pin works, or any utensil that will safely release anger) then roughly chop. Add the cucumber to a bowl with a big pinch of salt. Toss to combine, then set aside for about 15 minutes to release a good amount of water.

Meanwhile, combine the tahini, toum, yoghurt, coriander stems, lemon zest, a big squeeze of lemon juice and good splash of water. Season.

Heat a really good drizzle of oil in a large frying pan over a medium–high heat. Fry the falafels until golden brown and heated through, around 3–4 minutes. Add the dukkah and give it a good season. Toss to coat.

Drain the liquid from the cucumber and return the cucumber to the bowl. Add the white-wine vinegar and a drizzle of oil. Season well, then toss to combine. Top with a dusting of Aleppo pepper.

Spread the beetroot hummus over a serving platter and top with a drizzle of olive oil. Tumble the falafels over the top, then drizzle with some of the tahini sauce. Sprinkle the extra dukkah over the lot and top with the coriander leaves.

Serve the falafel with the pita, smashed cucumber and any leftover tahini sauce. Scoop and stack, etc.

✱ THE SUBS
TOUM garlic aioli
CORIANDER (CILANTRO) mint / parsley / a combination of
BEETROOT HUMMUS hummus of your choice
ALEPPO PEPPER sumac / sweet paprika / mild chilli powder

LECHE DE TIGRE LOVER

DF / GF

You may think this snack is over when the bowl is empty of kingfish, but look again. You'll see a small pool of liquid: that's leche de tigre (meaning tiger's milk in Peruvian). This prized liquid can be used for marinades, dressings and cocktails, or just sipped straight from the bowl.

Because classic Peruvian ceviche is typically served with boiled sweet potato, you'll be scooping with their crunchy chip counterpart, but feel free to use any other chip – corn chips are also a hit.

DRINK PISCO SOUR
SNACKS 2-4
COMMITMENT MINOR INVESTMENT

½ red onion, thinly sliced
60 ml (2 fl oz/¼ cup) coconut milk
zest and juice of 2 limes
1 habanero chilli, chopped
1 large garlic clove, chopped
bunch of coriander (cilantro), stems and
    leaves chopped separately
300 g (10½ oz) kingfish, cut into
    1 cm (½ in) cubes
1 avocado, peeled, stone removed, diced

TOPPERS
extra-virgin olive oil
corn nuts

SCOOPERS
sweet potato chips

Add the onion to a bowl with a pinch of salt and enough water to cover the onion (this will take out the intensity).

Combine the coconut milk, lime zest and juice, habanero, garlic and coriander stems in a bowl. Season to taste.

In a deep-ish serving platter or bowl, toss the fish in a good pinch of salt and give it a little rub. Pour the coconut dressing in, add the coriander leaves and avocado, and toss to coat.

Top with a drizzle of oil and corn nuts. Scoop with the sweet potato chips.

✱ THE SUBS
  RED ONION shallot / spring onion (scallion)
  HABANERO CHILLI long red chilli
  CORIANDER (CILANTRO) mint / basil
  KINGFISH swordfish / sole / snapper / sea bass
  CORN NUTS peanuts / toasted coconut
  SWEET POTATO CHIPS chip of your choice

SALSA THE DANCE

DF / GF

DRINK MOSCOW MULE
SNACKS 4–6
COMMITMENT MINOR INVESTMENT

60 ml (2 fl oz/¼ cup) fish sauce
1 chilli, thinly sliced
3 cm (1¼ in) piece ginger, peeled and
    finely grated
zest and juice of 1 lime
2 tablespoons neutral oil, like vegetable
    or sunflower
good pinch of sugar and salt
2 mangoes, peeled, stone removed, diced
1 avocado, peeled, stone removed, diced
140 g (5 oz) tinned crab meat
½ bunch of Vietnamese mint, leaves picked
½ bunch of coriander (cilantro), leaves picked

TOPPERS
crushed peanuts

SCOOPERS
prawn crackers

If you can hold fire on this until mango season, do. In cases of sheer desperation, I've made this with papaya and defrosted frozen mango. This swam perfectly well, but for it to really soar, wait to carve up those fresh and juicy cheeks.

On a serving platter, stir together the fish sauce, chilli, ginger, lime zest and juice, oil and the sugar and salt.

Top with the mango, avocado, crab and herbs. Toss to coat. Season with salt, if it needs any extra.

Top with crushed peanuts. Scoop it all with the prawn crackers. Done.

* THE SUBS
MANGO papaya / defrosted frozen mango /
peach / nectarine
TINNED CRAB MEAT chopped cooked prawns
(shrimp)
VIETNAMESE MINT mint / Thai basil
CRUSHED PEANUTS any form of salted peanut /
cashews

MANCHEGO-S WITH MANDARIN

GF / NF / VEG

DRINK FINO
SNACKS 4-6
COMMITMENT MINOR INVESTMENT

250 g (9 oz) packet microwave rice,
    cooked according to packet instructions
1 egg
2 tablespoons cornflour (cornstarch)
2 garlic cloves, finely chopped
bunch of basil, stems thinly sliced,
    leaves set aside
80 ml (2½ fl oz/⅓ cup) extra-virgin olive oil
4 mandarins (seedless if you can find them),
    peeled and chopped
½ red onion, finely chopped
60 g (2 oz) pitted Sicilian green olives, torn
80 g (2¾ oz) manchego, broken into chunks

If you have the time and minor foresight, this salsa can be made a couple of hours ahead (minus the basil). It means the manchego drinks in the extra oils and mandarin juice. That's up to you, but it's a worthwhile bonus.

FYI, Sicilian green olives do taste better off the pit, if you can be bothered. Use the side of a knife blade to crush the olives, then pull out the pit. Surprisingly less painstaking than it sounds.

Turn the grill (broiler) to high. Line a baking tray with baking paper.

Combine the rice, egg, cornflour, garlic, basil stems, 1 tablespoon of the oil and a good pinch of seasoning in a bowl. Give it all a good squish together with your hands. Press and spread over the baking tray to form a thin layer, about 25 × 30 cm (10–12 in) is a good size. Sprinkle with a little more salt and pepper.

Grill the rice 'sheet' until firm and starting to crisp around the edges, about 12–15 minutes, then use any utensil (a spoon works) or just fast hands to cut and tear the rice into cracker-sized pieces. Return to the grill and cook until golden and crisp, about 5 minutes.

Combine the mandarin, onion, olives, basil leaves and manchego in a bowl. Toss it all together with the remaining oil and season well.

Lay out the grilled rice pieces and get everybody else to spoon over their own salsa.

＊ THE SUBS
  MICROWAVE RICE any pre-cooked rice
  CORNFLOUR rice flour / plain (all-purpose) flour
  BASIL parsley / mint / dill / oregano
  MANDARINS orange family member of your choice
  GREEN OLIVES capers / olive of your choice
  MANCHEGO feta / pecorino / gouda / havarti / cheddar

GIMMIE GRIBICHE

DF / GF / NF

This wheel is rolling perfectly well. It needs no reinvention. This French sauce (gribiche) with steamed artichokes is a classic for a reason. Now go enjoy the gratification of chewing and tearing it off with your teeth.

If steaming artichokes feels like a task (it isn't, but I see why you would think that), asparagus spears and cooked prawns would also work with gribiche.

DRINK SEMILLON
SNACKS 4-6
COMMITMENT GO THE DISTANCE

3 eggs
1 lemon, zested
3 globe artichokes
2 garlic cloves, peeled
3 fresh bay leaves
3 anchovy fillets
90 g (3 oz/⅓ cup) mayo'
2 tablespoons capers, drained, rinsed and
    finely chopped
50 g (1¾ oz) cornichons, finely chopped
bunch of chives, finely chopped
small bunch of tarragon, finely chopped
1 heaped tablespoon dijon mustard

Either fill a steam pot (because we're steaming the artichokes later) or a large saucepan halfway with water. Bring to the boil. Add the eggs and hard boil them, about 10 minutes. Remove with a spoon.

Thinly slice half the lemon into rounds.

Now, tend to the artichokes. Using a serrated knife, trim the stems (leaving about 4 cm/1½ in intact). Slice off the top of the leaves, removing about 3 cm (1¼ in). Snap off any rough outer leaves and discard, including any on or near the stem.

Keeping the water rolling but reduced to a simmer, add the garlic, lemon slices and bay leaves. Fit a steamer or a colander on top of the pan and place the artichokes inside. Cover and steam until a knife slides easily into the centre of the largest artichoke, about 35 minutes.

Meanwhile, peel the eggs. Halve each egg and pop the yolks out into a bowl. Finely chop the whites, and set aside. Using a fork, mash and mix the cooked yolks, anchovies and lemon zest to combine.

Add the mayo', chopped egg whites, capers, cornichons, chives, tarragon and mustard. Check for seasoning.

To eat, snap off the artichoke leaves, dip into the gribiche and tear away with your teeth.

As you work your way through the artichokes, you'll eventually reach the tender hearts at the centre. Use a small spoon to scoop out and discard the fluffy looking choke. Now eat those total sweet hearts.

✱ THE SUBS
  FRESH BAY LEAVES dry bay leaves
  CAPERS green olives
  CHIVES / TARRAGON parsley
  DIJON MUSTARD wholegrain mustard /
  hot English mustard

LAZY MAN'OUSHE

VEG

I can't believe we exist in a reality where pre-made pizza dough can be bought from the supermarket. Even though it sits next to the basic packet soups (I still like you, minestrone), fresh dough feels quite 'restaurant'.

And because all dough is relatively the same and usually just a varying quantity of water and/or yeast, pre-made pizza dough can be used for so much more than pizza. Press it into flatbreads, shape it into little buns, roll it into stromboli, or make it into man'oushe (a Lebanese flatbread topped with za'tar). Five stars.

DRINK PALE ALE
SNACKS 6–8
COMMITMENT GO THE DISTANCE

500 g (1 lb 2 oz) pre-made pizza dough, at room temperature
flour, for dusting
40 g (1½ oz) za'atar
60 ml (2 fl oz/¼ cup) extra-virgin olive oil, plus extra for drizzling
400 g (14 oz) labneh

TOPPERS
pomegranate molasses (optional)
pomegranate arils
crushed toasted walnuts
pickled turnips
baby cucumbers, sliced lengthways
cherry tomatoes, halved
mint leaves

Preheat the oven to 240°C (465°F). Line a baking tray with baking paper. Now you have to wait – pour yourself a drink.

Divide the dough in half (if it isn't already in 250 g/9 oz portions).

Flour your hands and benchtop. Press and spread each portion of dough into a 20 cm (8 in) circle.

Combine the za'atar and oil in a bowl and give it a season. Spread the za'atar-oil mix over the dough circles, leaving a little border. Bake until golden and puffed, about 15 minutes.

Add the labneh to a serving bowl. Top with a drizzle of pomegranate molasses (if using), pomegranate arils, walnuts and an extra drizzle of oil.

Serve the man'oushe with the labneh dip, pickled turnips, baby cucumbers, tomatoes and mint. Tear. It. Up.

* THE SUBS
ZA'ATAR dukkah
LABNEH Greek yoghurt / sour cream / cream cheese
WALNUTS pine nuts / almonds / pistachio nuts
PICKLED TURNIPS any pickled veggies (if you even want)
CUCUMBERS & TOMATOES fennel / radishes / carrots
MINT LEAVES parsley / coriander (cilantro)

CLAMS ON HASH

GF / NF

Seafood and potato is such a reliable combination (fish and chips, duh). Grown in what seems like totally opposite environments (land vs sea), maybe it's this contrast that bonds them – just a theory. Working with that hypothesis, feel free to use the shellfish and frozen potato of your choice.

DRINK RIESLING
SNACKS 6–8
COMMITMENT GO THE DISTANCE

1 kg (2 lb 3 oz) frozen hash browns
2 tablespoons extra-virgin olive oil
2 shallots, finely chopped
6 garlic cloves, thinly sliced
bunch of parsley, stems thinly sliced,
    leaves chopped
250 ml (8½ fl oz/1 cup) white wine
1 kg (2 lb 3 oz) diamond clams
100 g (3½ oz) butter
zest and juice of 1 lemon, plus extra
    wedges to serve

Preheat the oven to 220°C (430°F). Line a baking tray with baking paper and lay out the hash browns. Bake for 20 minutes, or until golden brown. Season.

Heat the oil in a large saucepan over a medium–high heat. Stir in the shallot, garlic and parsley stems and cook for 5 minutes, or until the shallot has softened. Pour in the white wine, bring to the boil and reduce by half.

Add the clams and butter to the pot, bring back to the boil, then cover and leave to steam for 4–5 minutes, or until the clams have opened (there may be a few unopened strays, discard them). Remove from the heat. Stir in the parsley leaves, lemon zest and a spritz of lemon juice. Season.

Tip the clams into a serving dish. Tear the hash browns and stagger around the clams. Crack over some black pepper. Serve with lemon wedges and some forks, if you like. Have a shell bowl on the side.

★ THE SUBS
HASH BROWNS frozen chips / frozen wedges / frozen potato form of your choice
SHALLOTS any onion (brown / red)
DIAMOND CLAMS mussels

YOGHURT DIPS

Peppers & chickpeas

semi-dried tomatoes

chargrilled capsicums (bell peppers)

smoked paprika

torn parsley

crispy chickpea snack

Spinach & cumin

defrosted frozen spinach

crumbled feta

ground cumin

pickled jalapeños

fried garlic

Peanut & chilli oil

crushed peanuts

chilli oil

fish sauce

smashed water chestnuts

sliced spring onion (scallion)

Green olive & caramelised onions

caramelised onions

torn pitted green olives

anchovy paste

grated parmesan

toasted pine nuts

Spread the Greek yoghurt over a plate and top with the rest (stirring may lose you some visual appeal, if you care for that). Finish all with a drizzle of oil (a hint of garlic oil never did any wrong either).

All of these ingredients can be hand-torn, smashed or knifed. Again, don't forget to season. Well.

SHUCK ME

DF / GF / NF

It's textbook: oysters are best eaten freshly shucked. Like, shell off and necked (simultaneously appreciating the fresh and salty clean finish). How great is eating the sea?

I can appreciate not everyone is willing to sit down to a banquet of oysters, or even one or two, but the activity of shucking itself is shucking good! So, if someone's not too interested in the eating, let them feel involved and get them shucking. It's an aphrodisiac, so it'll get them going.

Sixteen oysters feels safe for four people (you do the math), unless you're Emily, who can eat beyond two dozen (yes, that's twenty-four) in a sitting. And if that's not enough, or you tire of shucking, get just enough to whet your appetite.

You'll need an oyster-shucking knife. They're cheap, easy to find, and you'll keep your fingers. Like with most activities, the more you do it, the better you get. It's oyster sport.

1 shallot, finely chopped
125 ml (4 fl oz/½ cup) red-wine vinegar
pinch of caster (superfine) sugar
16 oysters

TOPPERS
lemon wedges

Combine the shallot, vinegar and sugar with a good pinch of salt and a good crack of pepper. That's the mignonette.

Now, gather round with some tea towels (dish towels), the oysters and the shucker.

1. Fold a tea towel and wrap the oyster inside (this helps for gripping, stability and safety). Turn the shell flat-side up and leave the pointy tip of the oyster sticking out. Non-dominant hand caresses the oyster, the dominant one handles the knife.
2. Insert the pointy shucking knife tip into the pointy oyster hinge tip where the two shells meet. Start rocking the knife, up and down until you feel the blade easily pass through – the success lies in the rocking motion, so take your time, be patient and just keep rocking. Try different angles if you're struggling.
3. Once you've got leverage, twist the knife to release the two shells. You'll feel a satisfying pop. Euphoria.
4. With the shucking knife still in, gently run the knife along the top flat shell to detach the muscle that still hangs on, and open.
5. For slippability, run the knife around the edge of the oyster to release it then flip over for aesthetics. Such a pearl.
6. Spoon over some mignonette and/or a squeeze of lemon. Throw it back, master!

P&P PUNCH

POURS 12-16

Get out your biggest bowl. Be it a deep salad dish, massive soup pot or mixing bowl, all are perfect vessels.

This punch is all about the Ps, and the more the better. Pomegranate, pineapple ... I'll also take a ... patio, maybe a ... fire pit? Sure. Chuck it in, the bowl is big enough to fit it all.

And yes, you are likely to have some tequila left in a bottle, but wasn't that destined for something else anyway?

100 g (3½ oz) pomegranate arils
500 g (1 lb 2 oz) frozen pineapple
500 g (1 lb 2 oz) frozen raspberries
1.5 litres (51 fl oz/6 cups) tequila
500 ml (17 fl oz/2 cups) dry ginger ale
1 litre (34 fl oz/4 cups) pineapple juice
1 litre (34 fl oz/4 cups) soda water (club soda)
350 ml (12 fl oz) grenadine
3 limes, halved and juiced
bunch of mint, leaves picked
ice

Add the pomegranate arils, and frozen pineapple and raspberries to a large serving jug or bowl.

Pour in all the liquids, including the lime juice. Smack the mint and stir it all together.

Chill it all out with ice (the amount is up to you and your leftover vessel space). Ladle in, ladle out.

Carry at own risk.

✱ THE SUBS
  POMEGRANATE ARILS berry of your choice
  FROZEN RASPBERRIES berry of your choice
  TEQUILA vodka
  GRENADINE raspberry syrup

CHEESE
SLEAZE

Cheese can sometimes have the cheek to stick around, staying way past the last mouthful. Sometimes it comes back to bed and melts into a dream. Sends you to … Tahiti? Naked on the beach? Plaiting your guinea pig's hair? I don't know, it's your dream, not mine.

Speaking from personal experience, cheese dreams are more common with the softer-aged kind. Hard cheese and I get along in a different way – we're more 'in the moment' than 'meet you in bed later'. Both equally enjoyable.

But enough about me. As the good cheese sleaze I know you are, I want you to feel empowered to trade in the cheeses you sleep with. Do you take out taleggio? Come onto camembert? Rendezvous with Roquefort? Well, lock it in. Let your dreams run wild. Be a total sleaze about it.

Side note 1: there's a fair amount of parmesan flying around. Word of advice: hold onto the rinds and add them to soups, stocks, sauces and other liquidy brews. Leave to melt in for an always-appropriate parmesan lift.

Side note 2: there's quite a few wine pairings here. No doubt, it's a cheese sleaze's dear friend. If another variety of wine has your heart, ignore me and go with your gut.

NACHOS ITALO

GF / NF

One of my earliest memories? Mum picking me up from preschool, telling me bolognese was for dinner. Memorable because this only happened about three times a year; the simmer time and commitment to excellence was too crucial for my mum to throw it together on a whim. Respect.

In contrast, this version has been made with all iterations of ragu, from home-simmered to the hyper-convenient supermarket tub. All can be thrown together on a whim. Respect.

DRINK CHIANTI
SNACKS 2–4
COMMITMENT QUICKIE

230 g (8 oz) corn chips
200 g (7 oz) block parmesan
425 g (15 oz) bolognese sauce
60 g (2 oz) rocket (arugula)
drizzle of balsamic vinegar
drizzle of extra-virgin olive oil
250 g (9 oz) fresh mozzarella

TOPPERS
basil leaves

Preheat the oven to 220°C (430°F).

Spread the corn chips in a baking dish. Grate the parmesan on top, then bake until the cheese is golden and melted, 8–10 minutes.

Meanwhile, heat the bolognese in the microwave or a saucepan, whichever is the easiest.

Toss the rocket in the balsamic vinegar and oil. Season.

Spoon the bolognese over the baked corn chips. Tear the mozzarella over the bolognese and top with the rocket and basil. That's it.

✱ THE SUBS
PARMESAN cheddar / any good melting cheese
BALSAMIC VINEGAR white-wine vinegar /
sherry vinegar
MOZZARELLA bocconcini / burrata

FRIED TOMS ON RICOTTA

NF / VEG

As a callow juvenile, I used to munch on Cheds in the safe shelter of my parents' pantry. The same place I'd dunk my dirty eight-year-old fingers in Vegemite and honey (not simultaneously). But I'm grown up now, and holding a fantastically fragile glass of wine and buying Cheds with my own money.

FYI, Cheds are an Arnott's (Australian biscuit-making icon) cracker. No extra points for guessing, they're CHEDdar and pecorino flavoured. I'm bound by nostalgia, but use your favourite cheese cracker if you want.

DRINK ORANGE WINE
SNACKS 4–6
COMMITMENT QUICKIE

60 ml (2 fl oz/¼ cup) extra-virgin olive oil
500 g (1 lb 2 oz) heirloom cherry tomatoes
4 garlic cloves, sliced
½ bunch of marjoram, leaves torn or chopped
400 g (14 oz) ricotta
1 lemon, zested and cut into wedges

SCOOPERS
Cheds

Heat the oil in a large frying pan over a high heat. Fry the tomatoes until starting to turn golden and soft, about 4 minutes. Add the garlic and half the marjoram, toss to combine and cook until fragrant, about 1 minute. Give everything a good season, emphasis on pepper.

Meanwhile, dollop the ricotta onto a serving plate. Add the lemon zest and season. Mix and spread the ricotta over the plate. Top with the fried tomatoes. Lemon wedges on the side.

Scoop the ricotta with the Cheds. Spritz with extra lemon, if you feel.

✱ THE SUBS
HEIRLOOM CHERRY TOMATOES any cherry tomatoes will do
MARJORAM oregano / thyme
RICOTTA cottage cheese / mascarpone / crème fraîche
CHEDS cheesy cracker of your choice

G.O.A.T WALNUTS

VEG

It's a grand statement, but walnuts *can* get better. Call it lover's intuition. You've just got to (actually) butter them up, woo with a little honey, get handsy with some herby salt and serve with their soulmates: beetroot and goat's cheese.

DRINK SAUVIGNON BLANC
SNACKS 4–6
COMMITMENT QUICKIE

30 g (1 oz) butter
40 g (1½ oz) honey
200 g (7 oz/2 cups) walnuts
500 g (1 lb 2 oz) pre-cooked beetroot (beets)
6 thyme sprigs
1 tablespoon cracked black pepper
1 tablespoon sea salt flakes
1 teaspoon caster (superfine) sugar
150 g (5½ oz) goat's cheese with ash

TOPPERS
wafer crackers

DIPPERS
balsamic glaze

Preheat the oven to 220°C (430°F). Line a baking tray with baking paper.

Melt the butter and honey – the microwave will do. Spread the walnuts over the tray and pour the honey-butter mix on top. Toss to coat.

Bake the walnuts until golden and caramelised, about 10 minutes, tossing halfway through. Leave to cool for 5 minutes.

Meanwhile, cut the beetroot into wedges, or any bite-able size. Tear the thyme sprigs into a small bowl and add the pepper, salt and sugar. Mix to combine.

Sprinkle the thyme-salt mix over the walnuts and toss to coat. Tip the walnuts onto a plate, alongside the beetroot, goat's cheese, wafer crackers and a pool of balsamic glaze.

✷ THE SUBS
  WALNUTS pecans / almonds
  THYME rosemary
  GOAT'S CHEESE WITH ASH regular goat's cheese / feta / labneh

BREWED BOCCONCINI

NF / VEG

Bocconcini, so mellow, so fresh! But I'm a salt fiend, so let's add some.

Keep in mind – the bocconcini needs to marinate. It would love at least a good day to brew and absorb the other flavours. But if you're running late, one hour will do, just expect it to have less of a punch.

Ajvar is a Serbian roasted red pepper and eggplant relish. It's bold and smoky and best served even more liberally than tomato sauce, say, alongside grilled meats, roasted vegetables, on crusty bread or like here, as a dip, of sorts. You can find ajvar in most big supermarkets or speciality delis – and I hope you do.

DRINK PINOT GRIGIO
SNACKS 4-6
COMMITMENT QUICKIE

1 lemon
150 g (5½ oz) cherry bocconcini
½ bunch of basil, leaves picked
250 ml (8½ fl oz/1 cup) extra-virgin olive oil
4 garlic cloves, sliced or chopped
1 long red chilli, sliced or chopped
2 fresh or 4 dried bay leaves
250 g (9 oz) ajvar (see above)

SCOOPERS
toasted ciabatta

Peel the lemon rind with a potato peeler, then juice the lemon.

Add the bocconcini to a jar.

Bruise the basil (clap it in your hands) and add to the jar.

Heat the oil, garlic, chilli, lemon peel and bay leaves in a small saucepan over a medium heat for 3 minutes, or until just starting to bubble. Set aside to cool a little, around 5 minutes. Give it a good season.

Pour the oil over the bocconcini in the jar. Cover and leave to marinate in the fridge for at least 1 hour, but preferably overnight.

Spread the ajvar over a serving plate. Top with the bocconcini and some oil. Season again well. Serve with bread or just fork it.

* THE SUBS
BASIL parsley / mint
BAY LEAVES dried rosemary / dried thyme / can do without
AJVAR pesto / tapenade / chargrilled capsicums (bell peppers)

CHEESY-MITE POPCORN

NF / VEG

Romeo and Juliet **is cute and all, but how about a lengthy love letter to a chip? I'm not into those non-committal 'I think salt and vinegar is my favourite' (foul, by the way). I want to hear a passionate monologue on cut, thickness, brand (extra points for brand comparison) and seasoning complexity. Write or die for it, like those ill-fated youths.**

This is the recipe for my dearest cheddar chip. It's a love letter you can taste.

DRINK AMBER ALE
SNACKS 6-8
COMMITMENT QUICKIE

125 g (4½ oz/½ cup) butter
2 heaped teaspoons Vegemite
150 g (5½ oz) cheddar potato chips
100 g (3½ oz) salted popcorn
100 g (3½ oz) pecorino pepato, grated
bunch of chives, chopped or snipped

Melt the butter and Vegemite in a small saucepan over a low heat. Give it a little stir every now and then to help, about 4 minutes.

Tip the chips, popcorn and pecorino into a big serving bowl and toss to combine.

Stir the chives and a mad generous crack of pepper into the butter. Pour the butter over the chip-popcorn mix. Get your hands or spoon in and toss really well to coat.

Eat topped with another mad generous crack of pepper.

✱ THE SUBS
VEGEMITE Marmite
CHEDDAR POTATO CHIPS chip of your choice
PECORINO PEPATO regular pecorino / parmesan
CHIVES parsley / basil

BURRATA BITTERS

GF / VEG

DRINK CHAMBORD ROYALE
SNACKS 6–8
COMMITMENT QUICKIE

60 ml (2 fl oz/¼ cup) raspberry balsamic
    vinegar
good pinch of sugar
25 g (1 oz) currants
½ head radicchio, halved, leaves separated
½ fennel bulb, sliced
125 g (4½ oz) raspberries
2 burrata

TOPPERS
basil leaves
extra-virgin olive oil
toasted pine nuts

Quartering a radicchio and snapping away the leaves makes perfect bite-sized vessels. Just the right size to hold creamy burrata curd, sweet raspberries, crunchy fennel and a tangy dressing. Forget neat piling, let the toppings fall as they want.

Combine the vinegar, sugar, 1 tablespoon water and the currants – you'll only need a little bowl. Leave to sit and plump up for about 10 minutes (this isn't necessary, but it's nice).

Arrange the radicchio leaves on a large platter. Scatter the fennel over the radicchio.

Tear (yes, tear) the raspberries on top, in half is cute. Carry on the tearing with the burrata.

Spoon and scatter the currants (along with the vinegar) over the top, adding more vinegar if you want. Top with basil, a drizzle of oil and pine nuts.

You should know this by now: don't forget to season. Heavy on the pepper.

✱ THE SUBS
RASPBERRY BALSAMIC VINEGAR balsamic
vinegar / sherry vinegar
CURRANTS sultanas
RADICCHIO chicory (endive)
RASPBERRIES blackberries / blueberries /
strawberries
BURRATA mozzarella / bocconcini
BASIL parsley / mint
PINE NUTS almonds / walnuts / pistachio nuts

EDAMAM-ME-N-YOU

VEG

DRINK FRENCH 75
SNACKS 6–8
COMMITMENT MINOR INVESTMENT

300 g (10½ oz) frozen edamame pods
80 ml (2½ fl oz/⅓ cup) extra-virgin olive oil,
   plus extra for drizzling
1 heaped tablespoon fennel seeds
3 garlic cloves, sliced
30 g (1 oz) preserved lemon, finely chopped
1 tablespoon Aleppo pepper
300 g (10½ oz) stracciatella

TOPPERS
toasted pistachio nuts
basil leaves

SCOOPERS
sourdough

Preserved lemons are just lemons preserved in a hefty amount of salt. As the name mostly states. Therefore, imagine the taste to be intensely savoury with a prominent tang. Use sparingly. If they're not your jam (or preserve?), use lemon zest and juice instead.

When eating this *please* suck the pods. Hard. That's the flavour. Let's stay on theme and submit to finger licking.

Heat a big frying pan over a high heat and let it get really hot.

Add the edamame pods to the pan and cook until starting to get good colour, or better, until they start to char, about 5–7 minutes. Don't toss too much or they won't colour as well (not a massive problem though).

To the edamame, add the oil, fennel seeds, garlic and preserved lemon. Give everything a good toss and let it become fragrant, about 2 minutes. Take off the heat. Add the Aleppo pepper and toss again. Taste or gnaw on a pod and season as needed.

Spread the stracciatella on a serving platter. Top with the edamame, pistachio nuts, basil and a little more oil, if you'd like.

Have bread nearby to mop up the sauce. And napkins.

✱ THE SUBS
   FENNEL SEEDS caraway seeds / cumin seeds
   PRESERVED LEMON lemon zest and a spritz of juice
   STRACCIATELLA torn burrata
   PISTACHIO NUTS walnuts / almonds / pine nuts
   BASIL parsley / dill / mint
   SOURDOUGH bread of your choice

KIMCHI GARLIC BREAD

NF / VEG

Aversions to the smell of garlic confuse me (see rant on page 75 if you're interested). Again, I want to reiterate: wear the odour proudly. It's the perfumed result of a well-made snack.

As you would've guessed, that was to warm you up to the fact that there's a lot of garlic here. If you've got a garlic press, this is the time to use it, or you could just use garlic paste.

Remove the garlic smell from your hands by rubbing them over a cut lemon, if you don't want to be proper-nouned 'Garlic Girl'. (I have.)

DRINK SOJU
SNACKS 6-8
COMMITMENT MINOR INVESTMENT

150 g (5½ oz) butter, at room temperature
1 tablespoon gochujang (Korean red chilli paste)
2 spring onions (scallions), sliced
8 large garlic cloves, finely chopped or crushed
2 tablespoons toasted sesame seeds
1 sourdough bread loaf
300 g (10½ oz) vintage cheddar, grated
100 g (3½ oz) kimchi, sliced

Preheat the oven to 220°C (430°F). Line a baking tray with foil.

Combine the butter, gochujang, spring onion, garlic and toasted sesame seeds in a bowl. Give the mixture a season.

Slice into the bread loaf, not going all the way through (but almost) – enough to keep the base attached. Place on the tray. Smear the butter between all the slices, then shove in the cheddar and kimchi. Wrap the stuffed loaf in foil.

Bake for 15 minutes, then remove the foil and bake for another 5 minutes, or until the cheese is melted and golden.

Tear right into it with your hands. Garlic!

✱ THE SUBS
GOCHUJANG sriracha / chilli oil
GARLIC CLOVES 2 heaped tablespoons garlic paste
VINTAGE CHEDDAR regular cheddar / gouda / mozzarella / Comté / gruyere

EVERYTHING-BAGEL-BAKED-FETA

NF / VEG

I find feta's salty tang addictive. I also find bagels addictive. I *also* find baked beans (in all their forms) addictive. All separate encounters, but in the name of snacks, unite the trio.

DRINK CHENIN BLANC
SNACKS 4–6
COMMITMENT MINOR INVESTMENT

400 g (14 oz) tin butter beans, drained
100 g (3½ oz) semi-dried tomatoes
¼ teaspoon chilli flakes
1 lemon, zested and cut into wedges
a few thyme and oregano sprigs
60 ml (2 fl oz/¼ cup) extra-virgin olive oil
180 g (6½ oz) block feta
2 tablespoons everything bagel seasoning

TOPPERS
drizzle of honey

SCOOPERS
pita crisps

Preheat the grill (broiler) to high.

Spread the beans, semi-dried tomatoes, chilli flakes, lemon zest and wedges in a baking dish. Tear the thyme and oregano over the top. Drizzle with the oil and season well. Toss to coat.

Make a little space in the centre for the feta, turning to coat the cheese in the oil. Sprinkle the everything bagel seasoning over both sides of the feta block and press to coat.

Grill the feta until golden all over, turning halfway, about 10–12 minutes. Drizzle the honey over the top. Scoop with pita crisps.

✷ THE SUBS
BUTTER BEANS cannellini beans / chickpeas
SEMI-DRIED TOMATOES mixed olives / chargrilled capsicum (bell pepper) strips / fresh cherry tomatoes
THYME AND OREGANO rosemary
EVERYTHING BAGEL SEASONING mixed sesame seeds and garlic powder
PITA CRISPS cracker of your choice

PIZZA-ESQUE SAGANAKI

NF

Moving day. What gets you through? The inevitable takeaway. Because even if you've unpacked the pans, they need to settle into their new home just like you. Careful now though, takeaway in a new area is risky. And at times like this, you really need to be satisfied.

Emily and I punted a pizza joint and ended up ordering Bondi's finest hot salami pizza. Chance champions! Who even cares about unpacking when your hands are covered in salami oil and you're sipping Champagne?

I've also served this with bought pizza bases heated in the oven with a drizzle of oil. You could do that or just go full flatbread (as below). Either way, victory will be yours.

DRINK BAROLO
SNACKS 4-6
COMMITMENT MINOR INVESTMENT

2 × 200 g (7 oz) blocks haloumi
80 g (2¾ oz) pepperoni
250 g (9 oz) pizza sauce
olive oil, for frying
60 g (2 oz) honey
bunch of oregano

SCOOPERS
flatbreads

TOPPERS
grated parmesan

Slice the haloumi horizontally, then into large triangles. Slice the pepperoni (if it's not already). Heat the pizza sauce – microwave or a pan will do.

Heat a very generous drizzle of olive oil in a large frying pan. When the oil is hot, add the haloumi and pepperoni and fry until golden, about 2–3 minutes on either side. Drizzle with the honey and tear the oregano over the top. Turn (or toss) the haloumi to coat.

Either serve straight in the pan or tip onto a serving plate – up to you. Scoop the flatbreads through the pizza sauce and top with haloumi, pepperoni and grated parmesan.

✱ THE SUBS
PEPPERONI salami of your choice
OREGANO 1 tablespoon dried oregano or dried mixed herbs
FLATBREADS bread of your choice

SCRUNCHY FILO

NF / VEG

My favourite bit about anything butter-baked-filo is the crispy top layers. It's a full buttery chip! So, this is a pull-apart-party for that entire top layer.

Don't freak out about the deep baking dish, just act normal around it and eat this like nachos. Or just grab forks.

DRINK TOM COLLINS
SNACKS 6–8
COMMITMENT MINOR INVESTMENT

350 g (12½ oz) ricotta
zest of 1 lemon
3 garlic cloves, finely chopped
9 sheets filo pastry
100 g (3½ oz) butter, melted
200 g (7 oz) mozzarella, grated

TOPPERS
honey
parsley leaves
mint leaves
sumac

Preheat the oven to 220°C (430°F).

Combine the ricotta, lemon zest and garlic. Give it a good season.

Pull out a baking dish, around 20 × 30 cm (8 × 12 in). Brush a sheet of filo with some melted butter (or just spread it on with the back of a spoon). Sprinkle some mozzarella over the pastry, then loosely scrunch the filo with your hands and arrange in the baking dish. Repeat with the remaining filo sheets, butter and mozzarella. Drizzle any remaining butter on top. Dollop spoons of the ricotta mixture on top.

Bake until proper golden brown, about 20–25 minutes. Pull out of the oven and drizzle with honey. Top with parsley, mint and a sprinkle of sumac.

✱ THE SUBS
   RICOTTA cottage cheese / feta
   MOZZARELLA cheddar / haloumi
   SUMAC za'atar

IT'S ALL GRAVY

NF / VEG

This is kind of a Canadian poutine (pronounce: *poo-teen*): a hot chip, gravy and cheese curd combo from Quebec. Just with polenta-crusted wedges in place of the hot chips, a little more cheese, and a hot sauce to test everyone's limits. See? Uncanny resemblance.

DRINK DARK LAGER
SNACKS 4-6
COMMITMENT MINOR INVESTMENT

750 g (1 lb 11 oz) frozen potato wedges
2 tablespoons extra-virgin olive oil
40 g (1½ oz) polenta
1½ tablespoons garlic powder
40 g (1½ oz) parmesan, grated
200 g (7 oz) mozzarella, shredded
250 ml (8½ fl oz/1 cup) pre-made gravy
80 g (2¾ oz) caramelised onion relish

TOPPERS
chives
hot sauce of your choice

Preheat the oven to 220°C (430°F). Line a baking tray with baking paper.

Spread the wedges over the tray and toss in the oil. Sprinkle with the polenta, garlic powder and parmesan. Season well and give everything a good toss and press to coat. Bake the wedges until golden brown, about 25 minutes, giving them a flip halfway through.

Remove from the oven and scatter the mozzarella over the wedges. Bake for another 15 minutes, or until the mozzarella is golden and melted.

Meanwhile, heat the gravy and caramelised onion relish in a small saucepan over a low heat or in the microwave. Just make it hot.

Pour the gravy over the wedges. Scissor over chives. Splatter over hot sauce.

* THE SUBS
FROZEN WEDGES frozen potato chips /
frozen potato gems
PARMESAN pecorino
MOZZARELLA bocconcini / cheddar / gouda /
gruyere / melty cheese of your choice
CHIVES parsley / dill / a combo or none of these

CHEESY-CHOKES

GF

Buttery hollandaise is such an artichoke-people-pleaser. Baking those tender little marinated hearts on top of grated cheese forms a crunchy gruyere base. It's wild.

DRINK PROSECCO
SNACKS 4-6
COMMITMENT MINOR INVESTMENT

500 g (1 lb 2 oz) marinated artichokes, halved lengthways
3 garlic cloves, chopped
5 thyme sprigs, plus a little extra, torn
extra-virgin olive oil, for drizzling
150 g (5½ oz) gruyere, grated
150 g (5½ oz) hollandaise
1 lemon, cut into wedges
3 anchovy fillets

TOPPERS
toasted pine nuts

Preheat the oven to 220°C (430°F). Line a baking tray with baking paper.

In a bowl, toss the artichokes, garlic, thyme (save a little for garnish) and a drizzle of olive oil. Give it a good season.

Evenly sprinkle the gruyere over the oven tray and arrange the artichokes on top. Bake until the cheese is golden and crisp, about 20–25 minutes.

Meanwhile, spread the hollandaise over a serving plate. Spritz with some lemon juice. Tear the anchovies and scatter over the sauce. Smoosh the anchovies with a fork and mix to combine.

Top with the cheesy artichokes, reserved thyme, pine nuts and an extra crack of black pepper. Serve with the lemon wedges on the side.

✳ THE SUBS
THYME rosemary / oregano
GRUYERE cheddar / Comté / parmesan / pecorino
HOLLANDAISE aioli / mayo'
PINE NUTS almonds / walnuts / pistachio nuts

NOT AFRAID OF GORGONZOLA

VEG

Blue cheese is my *very* new friend. When I was interning at a food magazine, I sat in on a tasting for the 'best blue cheeses for Christmas'. Eager to impress, I was forced to channel my hatred inwards and inaudibly gag as everyone 'ooo'd!' and *salivated* over the pong.

Surprisingly, last year I experienced mass personal growth. I ate gorgonzola at a work cheese tasting and I actually enjoyed myself. Full circle? Could be. (This was at Penny's Cheese Shop in Kings Cross, Sydney. Go there.)

Repeat after me: 'I am not afraid of gorgonzola.'

DRINK MALBEC
SNACKS 6-8
COMMITMENT GO THE DISTANCE

200 g (7 oz) sheet frozen shortcrust pastry
milk, for brushing
1 leek
70 g (2½ oz) butter, cubed
2 tablespoons olive oil
handful of thyme sprigs
200 g (7 oz) gorgonzola
150 g (5½ oz) honeycomb
roasted walnuts

Preheat the oven to 220°C (430°F). Line a baking tray with baking paper.

Cut the pastry into small triangles, or any small cracker size you'd like. Arrange the pastry on the tray. Brush each piece with some milk (I've used my fingers as brushes in the past, you can too) and season with salt. Bake until golden, about 12–14 minutes.

Meanwhile, cut the leek in half lengthways, give it a little wash, then slice into small chunks. Spread the leek in a baking dish. Dot with the butter, drizzle the oil over the top and tear in the thyme (save a little extra for garnish). Give everything a good season and bake until tender, about 16–18 minutes.

Serve the gorgonzola with honeycomb, buttered leeks, walnuts and pastry crackers. Tear over the reserved thyme.

* THE SUBS
FROZEN SHORTCRUST PASTRY any cracker or bread you like
THYME oregano / marjoram / rosemary
GORGONZOLA Roquefort / Stilton / goat's cheese
HONEYCOMB regular honey
WALNUTS pecans / almonds / macadamia nuts

WINTER, WHENEVER

VEG

This feels fireside, even if you don't have one. Do you though?! Then wrap the chestnuts in foil or spread in a cast-iron pan and heat on the coals for about 20 minutes. So merry, so bright.

In general, chestnut-roasting time varies. Depending on their age and size, consider anywhere from 15–35 minutes a fair window. Base it all on them cracking open and smelling nutty. It's also easier to peel them while warm.

DRINK HOT TODDY
SNACKS 4-6
COMMITMENT GO THE DISTANCE

300 g (10½ oz) chestnuts
50 g (1¾ oz) butter
4 garlic cloves, chopped
4 rosemary sprigs, leaves stripped
pinch of nutmeg (optional)
250 g (9 oz) triple-cream truffle brie

SCOOPERS
fig-ish crackers

Preheat the oven to 220°C (430°F). Line a baking tray with foil. Boil the kettle.

Using a small knife (I like a serrated one for grip), score the skin of the chestnuts. One long strike makes them easier to peel, or mark a classic X. Add the chestnuts to a bowl and cover with boiling water. Leave to soak for 5–10 minutes, then drain and pat dry.

Spread the chestnuts over the tray and roast until the skin is starting to peel back, about 15 minutes.

Melt the butter with the garlic, rosemary and nutmeg (if using), the microwave is fine. If the brie didn't come in a baking-friendly box, crumple a square piece of baking paper big enough to hug and hold the brie and nestle the cheese in there.

Pour the melted butter over the part-roasted chestnuts and toss to coat. Add the brie in its baking paper nest. Return to the oven and roast for another 10 minutes, or until the brie is softened, the skin on the chestnuts is peeled back and it's smelling nutty.

Move the brie to a platter, for looks. Season the chestnuts and tip onto the platter too. Stab the brie, peel the chestnuts while warm and eat with those fig-ish crackers. Napkins needed.

✱ THE SUBS
ROSEMARY thyme / oregano
TRIPLE-CREAM TRUFFLE BRIE brie of your choice
FIG-ISH CRACKER cracker of your choice

CHEESE BOARD MATH

Manchego + melon + jamon

extras: green olives + marcona almonds

Goat's chevre + peach + bresaola

extras: basil + extra-virgin olive oil

Brie + blackberries + prosciutto

extras: balsamic glaze + walnuts

Blue cheese + fig + saucisson

extras: honeycomb + thyme

Good things come in threes, apparently. Take the holy trinity of cheese, fruit and meat. It's also really just straightforward logic. Math. Algebra. A + B + C = D(elightful).

Forgetting the math analogy from seconds ago, quantities actually feel futile here because these boards are meant to be organic, off the cuff. As for crackers, that feels like a personal shopping aisle decision, for you.

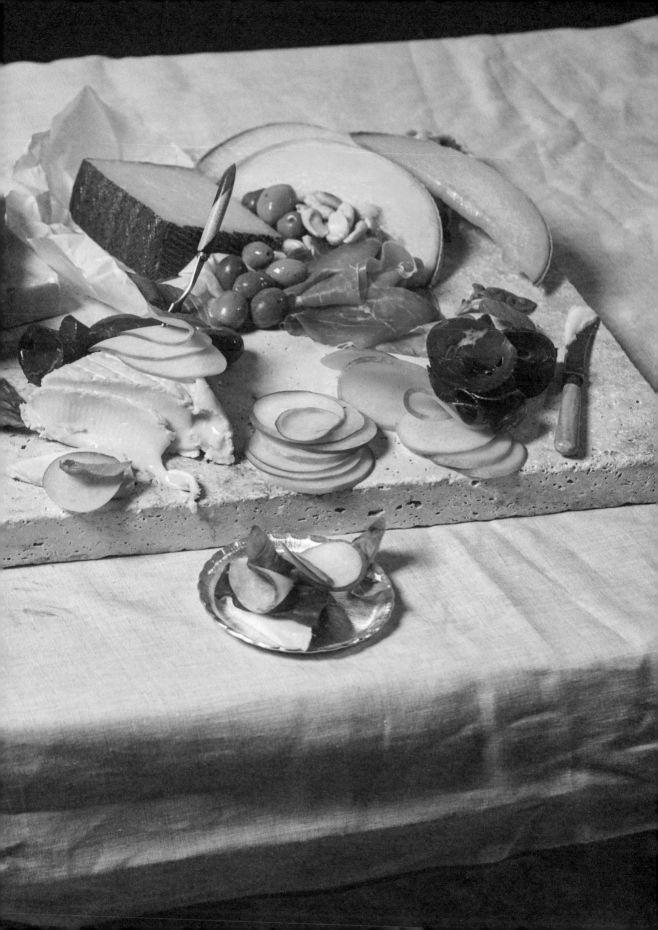

TEAM PASTA

VEG

In case the title isn't clear enough, let me clarify: you will not be tirelessly rolling out pasta yourself. You're just making the dough, and it takes minutes. There's also no pasta machine, you are the machine. Not that this is particularly strenuous. I mean, you're all just rubbing your hands together over drinks. What a pleasure!

The sauce is simple, because your efforts are being put elsewhere. So, if you can, using a good-quality pesto will make a big difference. You could also toss the pasta in your own favourite sauce instead – you're the chef.

250 g (9 oz/1⅔ cups) 00 flour
250 g (9 oz/2 cups) semolina, plus extra for dusting
600 g (1 lb 5 oz) pesto

TOPPERS
parmesan
basil leaves
toasted pine nuts
extra-virgin olive oil

In a large bowl, combine the flour and semolina with 250 ml (8½ fl oz/1 cup) water. When it comes together, use your hands to knead the dough until smooth. Kneading can be done in the bowl or on a board – whatever position you enjoy more. Cover the bowl and leave to rest on the bench for 30 minutes, can be longer.

When the team have assembled, grab that dough and dust a large tray or board with semolina, keeping the semolina bag on the side in case you need more.

Now, announce this to your sous chefs: (demonstration optional)

'No need to dust your hands with flour, just pinch off a little dough and rub and roll out between your hands to form a longish strand of pasta. It will end up being thicker in the middle and thinner at the ends. Make sure it's not too thick though.

Now, toss your little pasta in some semolina on the [insert: tray or board], and repeat, repeat, repeat! Yes, you're earning your feed.

If we could also make sure we keep the dough covered while we roll, that'd be great – just so it doesn't dry out, molte grazie.'

When you're done rolling and ready to cook, do this:

Bring a large saucepan of water to the boil over a high heat with a heinous amount of salt. Once boiling, add the pasta and cook until it floats to the surface and is tender with an al dente chew, about 5 minutes.

Use a large mug to grab out a good scoop of pasta cooking water, then drain the pasta. Return the pasta to the saucepan over a low heat with the pesto and a good splash of the pasta water. Stir, kinda vigorously, until looking emulsified, adding more pasta water if needed. Season and taste. Get the other rollers to taste too.

Tip the pasta onto a large platter, shave over the parmesan and top with basil and pine nuts. Drizzle some nice extra-virgin olive oil on top to finish. Shake hands with your team members for a job well done, then eat.

WE-GRONI

POURS 6

We're gonna get it on … our appetite on. Because that's what aperitifs do, thanks to their bitter edge. But I trust I don't need to tell you they're equally good whenever, wherever, forever.

2 blood oranges
90 ml (3 fl oz) Suze
180 ml (6 fl oz) Lillet Blanc
270 ml (9 fl oz) gin
ice cubes

TOPPERS
basil sprigs
soda water (club soda)

Thinly slice one of the blood oranges and juice the other.

Get a big jug – glass is pretty, but not essential. Add the Suze, Lillet Blanc, gin and orange juice. Give it a swizzle with a swizzle (or any utensil).

Now, add ice cubes to each glass along with a slice of the blood orange. Give the basil a smack with your hands and add some to each glass. Pour over the we-groni mix. Top with a splash of soda water.

✱ THE SUBS
  BLOOD ORANGES regular oranges
  SUZE Cocchi Americano Bianco / Luxardo Bitter Bianco / other Gentian liqueurs
  LILLET BLANC sweet white vermouth / St Germain

AFTERS, ALWAYS.

'Want to finish on a high? Come back to mine for dessert – it'll get handsy, in a good way.'

The promise! It pulls.

Like any prep for a promising night, most of the elements can be made ahead, so you can come home, crack open the fridge and get straight to it. Together. Because as with any relationship, these desserts are about equal effort. Get your people involved rolling things, pouring things, scooping things. It's the bare minimum.

Different to the others, these snacks have their liquor built into the recipes. A chewable digestif, if you will.

DOUGH-NUT DISTURB

VEG

Sure, the slow exiting ooze of jam or custard out of a doughnut is fun (not being sarcastic), but how about a spiked cream cheese frosting on top instead? I'm putting my thumbs up and so are you.

We're using bought cinnamon-sugar doughnuts, because I believe they are the finest form of doughnut on the shelves, but you can always double up on the ooze and use some jam- or custard-filled ones instead. No one's stopping you.

SNACKS 6
COMMITMENT QUICKIE

1 orange
250 g (9 oz) cream cheese
60 g (2 oz/½ cup) icing (confectioners') sugar
1 tablespoon milk
1 teaspoon ground cinnamon
2 tablespoons Frangelico
6 cinnamon-sugar doughnuts

TOPPERS
roasted hazelnuts and pistachio nuts
orange zest

Zest the orange then slice in half and juice.

Add the cream cheese, icing sugar, milk, cinnamon and Frangelico to a bowl. Using an electric mixer, beat the cream cheese until light and fluffy, around 2 minutes. Beat in some orange juice to taste.

Dollop some whipped cream cheese on top of each doughnut. Top with some nuts and orange zest. That's it.

* THE SUBS
  CREAM CHEESE mascarpone / crème fraîche
  FRANGELICO amaretto / Kahlua
  HAZELNUTS AND PISTACHIO NUTS walnuts / pecans / almonds

LEMON-SQUEEZE-ME

GF / VEG

This was originally imagined to be a build-your-own-tiramisu using sponge fingers for dipping. But, thanks to Emily's gluten aversion, I bought ricciarelli (an Italian almond biscuit) for her instead. Turned out, they were better. So much better.

As goes with drinking most things straight, quality is best. I was lucky enough to dip my (biscuit) fingers into my friend Adele's homemade limoncello. An angelic moment.

SNACKS 4-6
COMMITMENT QUICKIE

300 ml (10 fl oz) whipping cream
2 tablespoons icing (confectioners') sugar
zest and juice of 1 lemon
150 g (5½ oz) mascarpone
150 g (5½ oz) lemon curd
170 g (6 oz) tin passionfruit pulp

DIPPERS
limoncello
8-12 ricciarelli biscuits

In a bowl, whip the cream, icing sugar and lemon zest for 2 minutes, or until fluffy with soft peaks. Add the mascarpone and briefly beat until just combined.

Spoon the cream mixture into a bowl (a very silky experience). Dollop over the lemon curd and passionfruit. Give it a little swirl.

Pour the limoncello into glasses. Dip the ricciarelli into the limoncello then scoop into the mascarpone mix. Or just sip it straight. Or just experience it how you want to.

✱ THE SUBS
LIMONCELLO Cointreau / Grand Marnier
RICCIARELLI BISCUITS any nutty biscuit

NOT ANOTHER DECONSTRUCTED CHEESECAKE

VEG

SNACKS 4
COMMITMENT QUICKIE

250 g (9 oz) berries
a few thyme sprigs (optional)
125 ml (4 fl oz/½ cup) Chambord
250 ml (8½ fl oz/1 cup) crème fraîche
2 tablespoons icing (confectioners') sugar
1 teaspoon vanilla extract
zest and juice of 1 lemon
200 g (7 oz) Anzac biscuits

Deconstructed dishes get a slamming. But, if doing this is easier and gives the mouth the same result, can we agree to move onto bigger issues? Like cooking scrambled eggs with a whisk?

If deconstructing these cheesecake layers between glasses feels tedious, an arty display of splats on a big plate will also do nicely. See? Deconstructing rules.

In a bowl, combine the berries, torn thyme sprigs and Chambord. Set aside to let the berries absorb the liqueur, about 15 minutes. You can also prep this well ahead, like 3 days.

Meanwhile, add the crème fraîche, icing sugar, vanilla extract and lemon zest and juice to a bowl and give it all a vigorous stir.

Get four glasses. Spoon the crème fraîche mixture into the glasses, followed by the Chambord berries and hand-crushed Anzacs. Or layer it any way you want.

This can also be assembled ahead of time and refrigerated, if you feel up for it.

★ THE SUBS
THYME rosemary
CHAMBORD any berry liqueur
CRÈME FRAÎCHE cream cheese / mascarpone
ANZAC BISCUITS sweet biscuit of your choice

STICKY 'NANA

NF / VEG

It's a common tale. Ripe bananas equal banana bread. Common enough now that you can easily find good banana bread on bakery shelves, at cafes and even in nicer supermarkets. That's one job sorted. (I sourced gluten-free loaf, no qualms.)

The only thing to really do is channel a sticky date pudding state of mind. The canned whipped cream adds necessary theatre.

SNACKS 4–6
COMMITMENT MINOR INVESTMENT

4 medjool dates
50 g (1¾ oz) butter
2 slices banana bread
1 banana, peeled and sliced diagonally
60 ml (2 fl oz/¼ cup) date syrup
60 g (2 oz) tahini
60 ml (2 fl oz/¼ cup) maple syrup
1 teaspoon vanilla extract (optional)
30 ml (1 fl oz) shot whisky

TOPPERS
canned whipped cream

Tear the dates, toss the stones.

Melt the butter in a large frying pan. Add the banana bread and banana and cook until both bread and banana are golden on both sides, about 6 minutes.

Combine the date syrup, tahini, maple syrup, vanilla (if using) and dates in a small saucepan. Bring to the boil over a high heat and let the mixture bubble for a sec, then remove from the heat. Stir in the whisky and a good pinch of salt.

Slice the banana bread into thick fingers and arrange on a plate. Pour the caramel on top, then add the banana and a satisfying spray of whipped cream from the can. Perhaps some for your mouth, too?

✳ THE SUBS
DATE SYRUP extra maple syrup / honey
MAPLE SYRUP extra date syrup / honey / golden syrup
WHISKY rum
CANNED WHIPPED CREAM dollop cream

DIY TRUFFLES

GF / VEG

We're going to make ganache and we're totally chill about it. No one is sweating. It's just heating cream then stirring through the chocolate – simple. The rest is everyone just relaxingly rolling the ganache into balls for themselves – dipping the balls in things and rolling the balls in things. It's kind of messy, but it feels nice.

Here's a hopeful note on splitting: if the ganache does do this, just blitz it back together with a blender. It works. I swear.

Push the toppers out to any other form of nut, like pistachio nuts or almonds.

SNACKS 4-6
COMMITMENT MINOR INVESTMENT

150 ml (5 fl oz) thick (double/heavy) cream
50 g (1¾ oz) butter
2 tablespoons coffee liqueur
200 g (7 oz) dark chocolate, broken into pieces
100 g (3½ oz) milk chocolate, broken into pieces

TOPPERS
toasted coconut flakes
cocoa powder
cherries

In a small saucepan, heat the cream and butter over a low heat, swirling every now and then until the cream is starting to steam.

Add the coffee liqueur to the cream then pour the cream mixture over the chocolate in a bowl. Leave to sit for 1 minute. Now gently stir the chocolate-cream mix from the centre, nice and slowly with an occasional fold, until smooth and all the chocolate is melted.

Place a piece of plastic wrap on the surface of the ganache to prevent a skin forming. Chill until set, at least 3 hours.

Bring the ganache out of the fridge about 5 minutes before serving. Pass around spoons, scoop into the ganache and roll into balls. Roll the ganache balls in the coconut or cocoa powder, or even press the ganache around a cherry if you want. There are so many options.

✱ THE SUBS
COFFEE LIQUEUR Frangelico / nutty liqueur of your choice
CHOCOLATE all dark chocolate or all milk chocolate
TOASTED COCONUT FLAKES crushed nuts e.g. pistachio nuts / almonds / hazelnuts
CHERRIES berry of your choice

MANGO SEASON

VEG

What's the most wonderful time of the year? Getting a tax return. And summer's ripe fragrant mangoes. It's the thick, sweet and sticky juice dripping down your arm as you suck on the cheeks and pip. It's a moment to get lost in, leaning over the sink or bin. In saying this, I've made this dessert in winter with defrosted mango. Use this information as you wish.

This dessert works both hot and cold. As in, pre-made sitting in the fridge where it goes all trifle-like, or poured up hot in the moment. If you're pre-making, try piling it all into one large vessel and serving with spoons on the side.

We're making sugar syrup here and while you can also just buy a pre-made version, I thought this was a nice skill to have. Sugar syrup is used in many cocktails. Also use this information as you wish.

SNACKS 6–8
COMMITMENT MINOR INVESTMENT

100 g (3½ oz) caster (superfine) sugar
60 ml (2 fl oz/¼ cup) dark rum
600 ml (20½ fl oz) custard
½ teaspoon ground cardamom, or to taste
200 g (7 oz) white chocolate, broken into pieces
zest of 1 lime
200 g (7 oz) brioche, sliced
4 mangoes, peeled, stones removed, sliced

TOPPERS
toasted pistachio nuts

Heat the sugar and 100 ml (3½ fl oz) water in a small saucepan over a medium heat, swirling every now and then to encourage the sugar to dissolve. Simmer until slightly reduced and looking viscous, about 8 minutes. Stir in the rum.

Meanwhile, heat the custard, cardamom and half the white chocolate, stirring until the custard is hot and the chocolate has melted – either the stove or microwave works. Stir in the lime zest.

Now, toast the brioche and cut it into lengths.

Divide the brioche and mango between serving glasses – martini ones are cute. Snap the remaining white chocolate into smaller pieces over the brioche and mango. Pour in the sugar syrup.

Pour the hot custard over the bread and fruit in each glass, or just bring the jug to the table to make it buffet-style. Top with pistachio nuts.

✱ THE SUBS
DARK RUM rum of your choice
BRIOCHE challah / croissants
MANGOES 500 g (1 lb 2 oz) frozen mangoes / berries or stone fruit of your choice
PISTACHIO NUTS almonds / cashews

ICE-SCREAMING

Almost affogato

crostoli

hazelnut praline

cooled coffee

Extra virgin

tortas de aceite

extra-virgin olive oil

lemon zest

Waffle on

toasted waffle

raspberry sauce

basil

Could-be-breakfast

cornflakes

honeycomb

peanut butter

The melting mouthful that goes down like water, ice cream is textbook dessert-stomach food.

As I feel you're sorted for the classic toppings (e.g. Milo / whichever nostalgic sprinkle you're attached to), these are slightly more layered and textured, for your oral interest.

Use whichever ice cream you prefer, but I believe in a good-quality vanilla bean. Try topping these off with flaky sea salt. Really, do it.

HOW YOU FONDUE-ING

NF

One of the top search results for fondue is the 'rules', you know, 'fon-dues and fon-duen'ts'.

Imagine commandments like: *never* eat directly off the dipping fork, *never* pour from the pot onto your plate and *never* cut in front of somebody's fondue turn. Things this book would never condone …

There are also antiquated ones like if a woman loses her skewer she has to kiss all the men at the table. And if a man does, he has to provide the next bottle of wine. But just (fon) due what you want. Kiss the nearest person's foot and lick the spilled cheese off the table.

I know this feels like a Cheese sleaze chapter moment, but this is for the savoury dessert people. Those who like to finish their nights off with cheese instead of sugar. Or those who just stick to cheese. All night long, like Lionel Richie might.

250 g (9 oz) gruyere, grated
250 g (9 oz) Swiss cheese, grated
2 tablespoons cornflour (cornstarch)
300 ml (10 fl oz) dry white wine
2 garlic cloves, thinly sliced
juice of 1 lemon
1 teaspoon dijon mustard
pinch of ground nutmeg

DIPPERS
fruit: sliced pear / apple / grapes
bread: sourdough / rye / focaccia / ciabatta
meat: leg ham / charcuterie
veg': gherkin or any type of pickle / boiled potatoes /
  steamed cauliflower or brussel sprouts / cherry
  tomatoes / roasted mushrooms

Combine the cheeses and cornflour in a large bowl.

Add the wine, garlic and a good squeeze of lemon juice to a large saucepan. Heat over a medium–low heat until just starting to steam and lightly bubble. Very gradually, add a handful of cheese, stirring between each addition, adding more cheese when the last handful has melted. Lastly, stir in the mustard and nutmeg. Season to taste (the amount will depend on how salty the cheese is).

Bring the pot to the table and serve with the dippers. This will stay hot for around 15 minutes. If the fondue gets cold, reheat the pot over a low heat, stirring to re-melt.

FYI, when dipping, draw a figure of eight – this prevents the sauce from separating.

✱ THE SUBS
CHEESE fontina / gouda / cheddar / raclette
WHITE WINE vegetable or chicken stock
DIJON MUSTARD wholegrain mustard /
hot English mustard

CRACKING ICE

I am not saying this book wouldn't have been complete if a wine wasn't passed over while taking a mandatory think-over-the-garnish shower, if groups weren't force fed ('I know you don't like this, but eat it and tell me you like it'), or without Gita's dedication to finding fennel seeds in a small town. But, it was all fundamental fuel. To all those people, I want you to have the last cookie.

Hardie Grant team, publishing powerhouse, you materialised my imagination and made all this (ALL THIS!) possible. Michael, thanks for seeing the sparkle this book could have from the get-go. You got the vision and gave it gorgeous legs. Simon and Ana, you made the pages run (leap!) and always allowed *Happy Hour Snacks* to be its utterly silly self. Then there's Andrea's keen eye over all these pages, Daniel's top-tier illustrations and all the other Hardie Grant hands that have touched this. I can't emphasise enough thanks and gratitude.

Hey, shoot team, you're quite simply the best. Chris, Clare and Jaimee, you gave so much energy and care each day, happy to submit to the stick, splash and unavoidable modelling. You just got it! You're all so so so good at what you do and I'm so glad it was you three. And for all those special people who came to the group shoot day, that shoot team love includes you too.

Sush and Micky – thank you for letting us plunder and pillage your fun Bronte apartment, then proceed to cover it in shoot material, people and wet shoes. You're so generous, and I wish I was as cool and chill as you both. Sush, you again, thank you for all your fun crockery, letting us stain your tablecloths and for also just being you. Endlessly available to eat, discuss, expertly review, test and then make me clay pot rice when caught in the 'thick of it all'. You're the finger to my food.

Family. Gita, Clive, TJ, Andy and Spud. You all know anything and everything is absolutely nothing without you. You've shared in all the excitement and over-salting. I'm so grateful that Gita never missed a teary phone call, for TJ's constant bolstering and too-honest reviews, that we all enjoy the burn of hot English mustard, and that this probably isn't the best book for Clive and Andy who don't even like 'messy food'.

And friend-family – Em and Kate who cheerleaded the whole way. You listened to me talk this idea out on a long Friday beach walk and saw it through to submitting the manuscript in Greece, where you did the final read-throughs and gave all the appropriate giggles. You are in all of these pages, standing by with a glass of New Zealand pinot. Not to forget the fourth pillar, Pari, who holds hands so tight and slurps shellfish so well. No martini is quite as filthy as yours.

To the same Em, the steadfast steady hand (and wine passer! Bath drawer! Oyster shucker-er!), who was so happy to eat yet *another* experimental snack for any other weekday dinner, when all you probably wanted was a bowl of pasta to yourself – you're the truest, and flatmates.com.au deserves a bonus for introducing me to a sister.

To everyone who ate any even remotely book-related snack in those mildly forced tastings (not forgetting Culinary Kev, who also ran his bottarga-butter-based session). I'm so touched you came, chewed and reinforced what this book is all about. Here's the biggest hug, nah, squeeze!

For any bizarre words I may have mumbled, or incoherent encounters in the (SURREAL) writing delirium of 2023, it was only because my mind was off contemplating another way to make dips interesting – thank you to all the pivotal patrons, I hope it all makes sense now.

And hey, thanks to you too for buying this book! Please thrill and spill, because that's what this book is for, and showers. Bring a glass with you there too, may as well.

ABOUT THE AUTHOR

Despite being in and around the food industry since 2015, Bec Vrana Dickinson is still a blatant wearer of white who would rather taste salt levels with fingers than with spoons, and shred herbs with hands than with knives. With a diploma in Food & Wine and experience ranging from recipe development to content and copywriting, publishing and cheffing, Bec is now a Sydney-based writer and chef. Usually covered in oil stains, Bec will either want to know what you want for dinner, or how you take your whisky.

INDEX

Published in 2024 by Hardie Grant Books, an imprint of Hardie Grant Publishing

Hardie Grant Books (Melbourne)
Wurundjeri Country
Building 1, 658 Church Street
Richmond, Victoria 3121

Hardie Grant Books (North America)
2912 Telegraph Ave
Berkeley, California 94705

hardiegrant.com/books

Hardie Grant acknowledges the Traditional Owners of the Country on which we work, the Wurundjeri People of the
Kulin Nation and the Gadigal People of the Eora Nation, and recognises their continuing connection to the land,
waters and culture. We pay our respects to their Elders past and present.

A catalogue record for this
book is available from the
National Library of Australia

Happy Hour Snacks
ISBN 978 1 74379 997 0
ISBN 978 1 76144 140 0 (ebook)

10 9 8 7 6 5 4 3 2 1

Publisher: Michael Harry and Simon Davis
Head of Editorial: Jasmin Chua
Project Editor: Ana Jacobsen
Editor: Andrea O'Connor
Design Manager: Kristin Thomas
Designer and Illustrator: Daniel New
Typesetter: Celia Mance
Photographer: Chris Chen
Stylist: Jaimee Curdie
Home Economist: Clare Maguire
Head of Production: Todd Rechner
Production Controller: Jessica Harvie

Colour reproduction by Splitting Image Colour Studio
Printed in China by Leo Paper Products LTD.